T0152563

Barefoot in the Boardroom

Praise for
Barefoot in the Boardroom

"Barefoot in the Boardroom is clear and simple. No matter the industry, every leader or entrepreneur will benefit from the strategies. The framework demonstrates a step by step, yet agile, approach on how to lead through change. The business impact tools are practical and can be applied to any organization for quick wins."

—Dr. Stacii Jae Johnson, founder IWAGMU
& Femininity Lifestyle coach

"Very strategic and innovative. The success and sustainability of any team requires implementing relevant initiatives to accommodate new and improved outcomes. The customer of the future has pivoted to supporting businesses that reflect social and environmental initiatives, thus every organization should be evaluating methods to create impact, positive experiences, and profitability."

—Christina Dyer, CEO Positively Panache Gifts LLC
& Embellished Butterfly LLC

"Buy a copy for yourself. Then buy a copy for every leader in your organization. If you're looking for a change management method that works, you just found it! *Barefoot in the Boardroom* challenges leaders to look beyond "business as usual" and use innovative strategies to propel them forward."

—**Sheila Farr,** CEO at Gulf Coast Training
& Education Services, LLC

"*Barefoot in the Boardroom* provides effective change management strategies for both new and seasoned leaders. It's a must-read guide that can help you become an effective, impactful change leader!"

—**NaTonna Jones,** vice president, JPMorgan Chase

"*Barefoot in the Boardroom* is a must-read for leaders, executives, and change agents who are looking to achieve accelerated results within their organization. Shara's ability to simplify complex processes and techniques combined with her mastery of change management theory make this a profoundly useful book."

—**Tierra Womack,** founder at The Brave Way

"*Barefoot in the Boardroom* is a must-read for any business professional and/or company that is looking to expand their leadership skills, promote growth, and strategically set and execute business goals. Shara has set the bar really high by creating, documenting, and sharing her very own strategy blueprint that has a proven track record of success through her years of experience. Using this method you are sure to develop a productive team."

—**Alicia Jenkins,** CEO at Rock Me Fabulous

BAREFOOT
IN THE
BOARDROOM

EVERY LEADER'S GUIDE TO
NAVIGATING CHANGE

SHARA HUTCHINSON

NEW YORK

LONDON • NASHVILLE • MELBOURNE • VANCOUVER

Barefoot in the Boardroom

Every Leader's Guide to Navigating Change

© 2022 Shara Hutchinson

All rights reserved. No portion of this book may be reproduced, stored in a retrieval system, or transmitted in any form or by any means—electronic, mechanical, photocopy, recording, scanning, or other—except for brief quotations in critical reviews or articles, without the prior written permission of the publisher.

Published in New York, New York, by Morgan James Publishing. Morgan James is a trademark of Morgan James, LLC. www.MorganJamesPublishing.com

Proudly distributed by Ingram Publisher Services.

The information in this book was correct at the time of publication and the author intended to include all references. Therefore, the author does not assume any liability for loss or damage caused by errors or omissions. From the author's perspective, these are her memories and she has tried to represent events as faithfully as possible. Portions of this book are works of nonfiction. However, specific names and identifying characteristics were changed to protect the confidentiality of individuals and businesses.

Morgan James BOGO™

A **FREE** ebook edition is available for you or a friend with the purchase of this print book.

CLEARLY SIGN YOUR NAME ABOVE

Instructions to claim your free ebook edition:
1. Visit MorganJamesBOGO.com
2. Sign your name CLEARLY in the space above
3. Complete the form and submit a photo of this entire page
4. You or your friend can download the ebook to your preferred device

ISBN 9781631958120 paperback
ISBN 9781631958137 ebook
Library of Congress Control Number:
2021948629

Cover Design by:
Rachel Lopez
www.r2cdesign.com

Interior Design by:
Christopher Kirk
www.GFSstudio.com

Author photo by:
Steve's Creative Sessions

Morgan James PUBLISHING
Builds
with...
Habitat for Humanity®
Peninsula and Greater Williamsburg

Morgan James is a proud partner of Habitat for Humanity Peninsula and Greater Williamsburg. Partners in building since 2006.

Get involved today! Visit MorganJamesPublishing.com/giving-back

To all the leaders with whom I have had the privilege of serving while "barefoot."

Contents

Acknowledgments

I would like to begin by thanking my amazing husband, Todd. He was just as crucial to completing this book as I was, from listening to my spontaneous brainstorming sessions to giving me pep talks when I got discouraged to keeping our toddler entertained so I could write. You are everything I've ever wanted in a lifelong partner.

Second, I'd like to thank the entire team I had the privilege of working with at ARCOS for almost nine years. Working at a quickly growing start-up, with such innovative leaders, allowed me to gain practical experience that helped shape my leadership style. The year over year growth taught me how to scale teams through exponential change and pushed me to develop as a leader and continuously strive for next-level results while maintaining a positive culture. I cannot name everyone, but I'd like to acknowledge Bill Brackett. His leadership approach was that of a player-coach because he taught me how to handle circumstances and explained the "why" so that I could make strategic decisions on my own. We accomplished a lot as a team. He prepared me for the professional acceleration I experienced. Thank you, Bill, for teaching me how to be more succinct, for pushing me to reach seemingly unachievable objectives, and for genuinely caring about my well-being.

Occasionally you get the opportunity to work with someone who profoundly influences you both professionally and personally. Ross Fuller, my mentor/coach, deserves special recognition. I had no idea I would end up telling you about my life story in the middle of a business trip when we traveled to the Iowa office to discuss our department's growth strategy. You were probably one of the first people to help me see the correlation between my life experiences and my leadership growth opportunities. You taught me to "allow work to get done through me and not by me" via the power of trust. Thank you for always asking me tough questions and then holding me accountable for the answers.

I am also thankful to my VISTAGE Leadership Group for allowing me to use the group as a personal learning laboratory. What an incredible joy it is to meet six times a year with individuals who are genuinely interested in ideas, who give constructive feedback on any topic, initiative, or technique that comes before them, and who are constantly willing to try out new principles and ideas.

A special thanks to our VISTAGE chair, Perry Maughmer. You push me to reach my full potential and challenge me to challenge myself. I appreciate your honesty and transparency. Your love for books and willingness to share titles that have helped you elevate your leadership inspired me to read some of those same books and be enlightened. Thank you for partnering me with Brian O'Riadon as my mentor. I feel you put thought into who you assigned to me. My time with Brian was invaluable and encouraged me to audition and land my first TEDx talk. Thank you, Brian, for giving me the hourglass and the book, *The Traveler's Gift*. The hourglass is my daily reminder that I am the manager of my own time. You may be happy to know that I keep both the hourglass and the book on my desk.

Last year during the COVID-19 pandemic, I had the chance to meet and receive personal coaching from Forbes Riley. I met her backstage during a virtual event we both spoke at. During our session, she asked me a question that changed the trajectory of my life. She asked me, "Shara, what do you want?" I gave some generic answers, and then she followed up by asking, "What do you really want?" At that moment, I felt like a lump was in my throat because I realized that even though many already saw me as a success, I had greater potential. She helped me know that I can have so much more as long as I am willing to ask for it. Thank you for remaining in contact with me and for connecting me with Steven Samblis. That unlocked the opportunity for me to co-author two books with over one hundred other authors. I admire you for being vulnerable and approachable. You taught me to perfect my pitch and deliver it with confidence. Thank you.

I must also show appreciation to my parents. Thank you both for your support during all my accomplishments as well as my moments of failing forward. Dad, you exemplify all the leadership qualities I mention in this book. I admire your dedication to the church as well as your ability to remain relevant while maintaining your convictions. In over twenty-five years of ministry, you have experienced change, chaos, and comfort, yet you maintained a culture of growth and commitment to the vision. You demonstrate what it means to be "barefoot." Mom, you always push me to be the best version of myself. When I attempt to avoid situations or topics that may be uncomfortable, you encourage me to face my fears and remind me that you are always there if I need to talk. You always share how proud you are of me, motivating me to continue working toward my next level.

I appreciate everyone who provided me with thorough and helpful feedback on this book. You generously contributed your time to examine the text and encouraged me to clarify concepts, research specific aspects of my points, and explain the rationales for certain conclusions.

Thank you to my publisher, Morgan James, and the entire team there for helping me take my book far and wide to help others on their professional and personal journeys.

Lastly, without the corporations and individuals who allowed me to explore and test strategic leadership theories over the past decade, as well as the various speaking engagements, coaching sessions, mastermind meetings, training, workshops, and consulting engagements, this book would not have been conceivable.

Foreword

'm often asked, as a successful TV personality and CEO of a multimillion-dollar empire, were you always self-confident and successful? This is funny to me because my motto is "You are the sum of the obstacles you overcome," and the truth for me is that I started as an overweight, self-conscious, awkward little girl with a broken nose and frizzy hair who wore braces for eight years.

My childhood was lonely and confusing, and then my dad spent three years in the hospital because of an industrial accident. I was withdrawn, quiet, and often ashamed to be seen, until I unearthed the real me. Through mentorship and maturity, I went on to appear in movies and on TV, act on Broadway, host several game shows, write best-selling books, interview rock musicians on one of the country's largest radio stations, launch a profitable fitness empire, and generate $2.5 billion in product sales from thirty years on home shopping shows and 194 infomercials. This journey helped establish me as an industry pioneer in cable TV. Through perseverance and tenacity, I even turned the table on my childhood bullies and, in 2010, the same girl who was tormented for being overweight and awkward was inducted into the National Fitness Hall of Fame. How did that happen? I shattered every limiting belief, stepped outside of my comfort zone, and decided to fulfill the dreams I had as a little girl.

One of the most memorable of my accomplishments was when, while speaking in front of over ten thousand people at a conference sponsored by Grant Cardone, I kicked off my shoes and raced across the stage barefoot. It was a freeing and unexpected moment that people still talk about years later! Sometimes you must do something out of the ordinary to experience extraordinary results.

Shara and I first met at a conference where we both spoke. Following that, we not only had the opportunity to co-author two best-selling books with a number of other authors, but I had the honor of having her enrolled in my training and got to serve as a mentor to her.

In my world, where I interact with thousands of people, Shara is a shining star who just needed a gentle and loving nudge from someone who has walked down the road she is heading down. Her journey as a mom is similar to mine, and the sparkle in her eye now shines even brighter. She is a genuine leader who navigated the corporate world but managed to place a high value on keeping customers and employees happy in order to achieve critical objectives. She is a creative thinker who is willing to challenge the status quo when necessary to ensure the sustainability of an organization. It's no surprise that she would write an inspiring book titled *Barefoot in the Boardroom*.

Behind most failed businesses are leaders who refused to diversify and adapt to changing times. In order to maintain my level of success throughout my career, I've had to change my company strategy and offerings many times. When the COVID-19 pandemic struck last year, my whole business was thrown into disarray, and the only way I was able to make over a million dollars when I couldn't travel for speaking engagements was to pivot and establish virtual service offerings. This was entirely foreign to me, but I had no choice but to go "barefoot" and do something I had never done before.

This book appeals to me because it helps leaders and entrepreneurs define their most ambitious goals, provides a comprehensive framework for navigating the change necessary to accomplish those goals, and equips you with the tools necessary to lead through the unexpected.

Barefoot in the Boardroom is more than just a collection of methods. This approach is founded on a strong basis that gives a meaningful response to the frequently ignored question: How do I successfully lead my team through change? The concepts in this book are based on Shara's extensive experience assisting leaders and leadership teams in overcoming the typical and reoccurring obstacles that affect our culture's leadership blind spots. These techniques will equip you with the tools to enhance your own level of success and the performance of your team by developing employees who want to follow you rather than employees who feel obligated to do so.

Shara and I have at least two things in common: we both care about developing and uplifting people, and we're both willing to give a presentation without wearing shoes. Now it's your turn. Take your shoes off and go "barefoot in the boardroom."

Here's to your success!

Forbes Riley,
celebrity TV host, motivational speaker,
and transformational success coach

Preface

Barefoot in the Boardroom is the brainchild from a day when I had to decide to remove my shoes just before a corporate presentation I was scheduled to deliver. Due to the excruciating pain my feet were in from walking in high heels all day, I decided that the only way I could successfully share the strategies and insights without distraction was to be barefoot. My boss at the time looked at me and said, "Hmm. You are barefoot in the boardroom. That is a book title." He did not know it at the time, and neither did I, but he would later inspire this book title. Years later, after working to help many organizations navigate change, I reflected on that moment and realized the correlation. Sometimes in business, pain forces you to do something unorthodox to get the desired result. You cannot be so concerned about people looking at you or wondering why you've "stepped out of the box" that you forfeit the desired result.

Who Is This Book For?

I have written this book specifically for leaders and managers in the business world as well as small and medium-sized organizations. However, with larger corporations, nonprofit organizations, churches, and any industry that wishes to succeed in the long run, the principles would still apply.

Read and sincerely focus on the values in this book. You will have a fresh understanding of the influence corporate culture has on every department and every outcome. These insights will enable you to make a strong connection between your business plan and your strategy for people to support the company long-term.

Why Should You Read This Book?

This book is a guide that is useful alongside your strategic planning initiatives. It is not simply meant to be read, but rather to produce actionable insights that create results. If you apply the actionable steps and methodologies in this book, you will develop as a leader, and you will also encourage the development of other leaders. As a result, you will scale your organization, team, or department to not only identify the right strategic initiatives but to execute those initiatives and sustain success.

This book has three parts:

1. You're Already in the Boardroom
2. Take Your Shoes Off
3. Stand on the Table

In the first section, "You're Already in the Boardroom," you will learn why it is critical to future-proof your organization or department and expose yourself to new ideas as a leader, and you'll also get introduced to my signature EXPOSEYOUR™ Leadership Capacity approach. This approach includes the nine leadership competencies needed to develop a high-performing team and information about having a personal development plan to get to your next level in leadership.

In the second section, "Take Your Shoes Off," you will cast your vision. You will discover how to align your business strategy with your people strategy to ensure you have the right people in the right seats to get the right results. Once you understand how to build and scale your team, we will talk about innovating customer service. If you don't delight your customers, you will eventually drive them away. If you drive them away, that will negatively impact the bottom line.

In the third section, "Stand on the Table," I will introduce the BAREFOOT Method™, my signature change management strategy that you can apply to your organization, team, or department to ensure it is sustainable. Lastly, you will identify and operationalize your next steps.

This book will challenge you to break out of your box to innovate with the times. You'll gain clarity about your strategic initiatives, key objectives, operational tactics, and measurable outcomes so you don't end up like one of the leaders or organizations who failed to implement changes to sustain longevity.

So go ahead, take your shoes off, and get ready to walk barefoot in the boardroom.

Introduction

"Barefoot in the boardroom." What does that even mean? The story behind this phrase inspired me to write this book—it was a scenario that caused me to look at the traditional view of leading a successful business or department and then do the opposite.

> "Management is efficiency in climbing the ladder of success; leadership determines whether the ladder is leaning against the right wall."
>
> —Stephen Covey

I have attended and facilitated several board meetings throughout my career, presenting my ideas to others—a drill of corporate work, you might say.

You know what the presentations are like and how they take a toll on your back (at the very least for us ladies). Imagine being dressed in crisp clothing with your feet donning high heels and having to stand for an extended period. Guess what? After several hours, those same heels will shoot a sharp pain straight up your legs and through your back, yet you must plaster a smile on your face and own the meeting if you want to be effective. You look the part, but deep down inside you want to scream.

Now that I have set the scene, I will tell you how being barefoot in the boardroom exposed the structure used by the world's greatest leaders and managers to protect their organizations for the future. A few years back, I presented a strategic plan at an organization. I had been walking in heels all day, so by the time the meeting started, my feet were throbbing. They were hurting so badly that I didn't know whether it would be more painful to keep my shoes on or take them off. It felt as if my toes were on fire and I had no extinguisher. I just wanted to sit down, but since I was leading the meeting, I couldn't. As the meeting began, my feet ached so badly that I had no choice but to take them off. In a corporate environment where this might seem unprofessional, imagine the overwhelming pain that compelled me to take off my shoes. But that's precisely what I did. Initially, people snickered and gave me the "look," but as I discarded the looks along with my shoes, I soon lost myself in my presentation. And no one even batted an eye once I started discussing key objectives, operational tactics, and measuring the desired outcomes. The meeting was a success! By the end of it, no one, not even I, cared that I was not wearing shoes. I had stepped out of my comfort zone despite what others thought, and it worked.

That was when I realized that this "unprofessional behavior" was nothing more than a norm. The pain caused by wearing those heels was so great that I was willing to endure the pain of changing my behavior. I had an "aha" moment.

> As leaders, we should not allow norms to hold us back, because sometimes the only way to avoid ultimate pain is to instigate rapid innovation.

You have to do things out of the ordinary to achieve the desired results and scale your business, department, or team. As I reflect, I know I would not have given that presentation 100 percent if I had still worn my heels. The pain would not have allowed me to do so. With this thought in mind, I present to you *Barefoot in the Boardroom*.

> "You never change things by fighting the existing reality. To change something, build a new model that makes the existing model obsolete."
>
> —Buckminster Fuller

Phase 1

You're Already in the Boardroom

Chapter 1

Time for a Change

*"They always say time changes things,
but you actually have to change them yourself."*
Andy Warhol

I magine this. You're standing on top of a ten-thousand-foot
building. You look down and realize you're able to zoom audi-
bly and visually into the second-floor boardroom—meaning
you can hear and see everything going on. In this boardroom,
you and your entire leadership team are having a strategic planning session about the organization's future. More specifically,
your twenty-five-year plan. What are you talking about? How is

the conversation going? Who from the team is offering out-of-the-box ideas? Has anyone brought up how things may change in your industry and with technology over the next five years, ten years, or twenty-five years? Have you determined how you will adjust to these changes? Based on your conversation, will your organization still be around twenty-five years from now? Is your plan future-proof?

You're reading this book because you've already reached a certain degree of success, and now you're aiming for the next level. However, the next level comes with next-level challenges, and you recognize that what you have done to get here won't get you there. The question you are facing is, how can you level up your leadership to ensure the longevity of the business? The answer is simple, but not easy: *change*.

All organizations experience change. Some people are more threatened by the pace of change than the actual change itself, and others oppose change because they feel insecure during the awkward phase of confusion between the old normal and the new normal. This analogy or example to go barefoot in the boardroom explains the importance of adopting changes as you grow. It permits you to do something out of the ordinary to achieve extraordinary results.

Anything around us can change, move, and need creativity over time. Suppose you refuse to anticipate and forecast the future because you are trapped in the old ways. In that case, you will miss opportunities and experience the same pain my feet and back felt before I took my shoes off in that board meeting—only you'll feel it in your key performance indicators (KPIs).

> "Times and conditions change so rapidly that we must keep our aim constantly focused on the future."
>
> —Walt Disney

No leader with an audacious vision builds a company with the intent of only surviving for a few years. The objective is to keep growing and reach the heights of success over time and have a future. For that, a plan and having the right leaders in the right positions is necessary.

For a business to grow in an ever-changing environment, a leader must consider all the factors that impact business performance and develop strategies accordingly to make the business plan future-proof.

Change is the leading force in the corporate world that decides the decline or rise of a company, so get comfortable with it and get ready to take your shoes off!

What is Future-Proofing?

Future-proofing is the process of forecasting the effects and shocks of potential disasters that might cause a company to go out of business or suffer financially. Based on these expectations, leaders develop methods to minimize the repercussions for the business. There are four basic principles for reducing the impact of future shocks:[1]

1. Create a well-structured framework.
2. Establish a solid financial foundation for your company.
3. Do not overlook the importance of putting your plans into action.
4. Formulate a strategy.

Why Is It Important to Future-Proof?

In the business world, there is a lot of competition. Furthermore, globalization has resulted in incredible technological and economic developments, making the playing field unpredictable and unequal. Whether it's a new technology, technique, or product, something new enters the market that poses a danger to your company every day.

Organizational success and survival are highly reliant on the capacity to manage and adapt to change. As a result, businesses must establish a long-term strategy beyond prior techniques, approaches, and quick fixes. This entails planning for the future, looking beyond the confines of the internal business environment, and considering the entire industrial ecosystem in which the company operates.

All You Need Is a Hedgehog

Typically, a long-lasting business is not an overnight success. Instead, its executives spend time planning to reinforce the business foundations to ensure its long-term success. To do this, they work to understand their "Hedgehog concept," or "secret sauce" as I call it, which makes their business unique. I read an article that explained this concept well as it relates to leadership and business.[3] Here is an excerpt:

"The term 'Hedgehog' comes from the famous essay by Isaiah Berlin titled 'The Hedgehog and the Fox.' The story contrasts the fox as a cunning animal who knows many things, always seeing the world in all of its complexity, with the hedgehog who knows one big thing really well and simplifies a complex world through a single organizing idea.

"As it relates to business, fox companies recognize and pursue every opportunity, seeing the world in all its complexity. They work to be good at many different things so that they can take advantage of opportunities as they are presented. They become scattered and diffused, never really becoming great at any one thing. Hedgehog companies, on the other hand, are laser-focused, understanding and concentrating on what they are best at. They are able to simplify a complex world into a single organizing idea, always considering first whether or not an opportunity fits into their pattern of success."[2]

Considering the above, what is your Hedgehog concept? What does your organization need to focus on to be future-proof? The article went on to outline three questions you must be able to answer to understand your Hedgehog concept:

1. **What can you be the best in the world at?**

   Consider what would happen if you concentrated all of your energy and effort on a single goal. What might you become the most extraordinary in the world at? It's not that you're establishing a goal to become the greatest at anything; it's that you know what you're capable of being the best at. It's also critical to recognize what you won't be able to improve at.

2. **What drives your economic engine?**

   The answer demands a comprehensive grasp of the one element that causes you to make more money than any other ratio or denominator in your company. Thinking outside the box of your industry's obvious KPIs may lead to significant creative breakthroughs, separating you from the competition and potentially upsetting the status quo.

3. **What are you deeply passionate about?**

A company's employees must be dedicated to and interested in their job for it to be successful. This necessitates both their emotions and their brains being engaged. Understanding the goal of your company and your employees' interests and being persistent in pursuing opportunities that align with those purposes and passions is a crucial element of comprehending your Hedgehog concept. The idea is to make a conscious decision to do the job that naturally inspires enthusiasm in your workers rather than striving to get them enthused about their work.

Answering these three questions will set you on the path to creating a ten- to twenty-five-year vision that will propel you to the next level to be an innovative leader. In later chapters, we will discuss this in more detail.

Innovative Leadership Matters

If you do a little research, you'll discover several examples of organizations that collapsed because they failed to see the necessity of future-proofing their operations. The majority of these companies were highly successful and dominated their respective industries. Despite being at the top, they were unable to sustain their market positions. The reason? Failure to innovate. Why did they fail to innovate? Leadership.

> "The task of the leader is to get their people from where they are to where they have not been."
>
> —Henry Kissinger

Blockbuster, one of the largest DVD rental companies, is an excellent illustration of the inability to innovate.

> "Innovation is the unrelenting drive to break the status quo and develop anew where few have dared to go."
>
> —Steven Jeffes

Blockbuster vs. Netflix

One of the most well-known DVD rental companies was Blockbuster. However, because of its inability to adapt to change, it is frequently presented as an example of a company left behind by disruptive innovation. With hundreds of locations throughout the world, it was a market leader in the video rental industry. Until video streaming came along, it was at the top of the business. One article aptly explains Blockbuster's fatal mistake.[3] The gist of the article is as follows:

Because they failed to innovate with their digital offerings, the company, with its costly rents and overhead, began to lose ground to DVD postal services and early-stage streaming services such as Love Film.

To make matters worse, because of their market position, Blockbuster had the chance to buy Netflix—a young firm that offered postal video services. Netflix would sell 49 percent of the company and adopt the Blockbuster branding. However, the leader decided not to. They never saw a future of streaming, so despite having the opportunity to purchase Netflix on several occasions, Blockbuster decided to continue doing what they had always done. Now Netflix dominates the sector and Blockbuster is left behind.

This example explains why it is vital for companies, small or big, to build a system that can help them anticipate the future. Rather than focusing on short-term solutions, companies need to calculate future risks and prepare to tackle them in advance. If Blockbuster had considered this fact, Netflix would not have introduced streaming services in the market. The changes could have been an opportunity for the company to grow. Instead, their lack of change led to their failure.

The CEO of Netflix, Reed Hastings, said: "If Blockbuster had launched their streaming service two years earlier, Netflix may never have happened."

Blockbuster was only one of many examples. Aside from competitors, executives are occasionally caught off guard by events that drastically disrupt their business and the whole economy. The COVID-19 pandemic proves this. Many companies were seriously affected, with some industries suffering more than others. While there were essential businesses that remained open based on the necessity of their products or services, many companies did not fit into that category. Some could not have done much to minimize the impacts. However, others could have mobilized their staff, continued operations faster, and increased sales had they noticed the trend of mobile services, remote-work technology, and digital innovation two years earlier.

> "The greatest danger in times of turbulence is not the turbulence—it is to act with yesterday's logic."
> —Peter Drucker

COVID-19 Has Taught Us to Innovate Digitally

Businesses may learn a lot from the year 2020. Many companies had to discover new methods to adapt and stay relevant due to the coronavirus pandemic. Companies in the manufacturing, entertainment, and food industries, as well as schools and churches, all had to socially distance their members and employees. The economy felt the effects. People couldn't interact in the same way anymore. Therefore, everyone had to discover new methods to connect for business and social activities. With so many standards, dealing with lockdowns and implementing standard opening procedures (SOPs) for safety with a small team was tough. This pandemic served as a reminder of how unpredictable the future is and how organizations must be proactive to survive unexpected events. The world had to embrace digital innovation. School-aged children were required to take online courses. Everyone had to adjust to the new norm and find ways to be effective. I was used to working in the office with my staff and had to learn ways to lead an entirely remote workforce.

COVID-19 caused numerous companies to relocate their operations to their staff's homes to prevent the disease from spreading. This transition, however, was not simple for all organizations. Businesses had immediate difficulty providing secure system access to their employees because they were not prepared to handle the unexpected demands of digitizing their processes. In-person meetings, paper-based transactions, travel, and other routine activities are examples of these processes.

Alongside the businesses that had a difficult time running their operations during the pandemic were some who could respond to the changes. These businesses thrived during the pandemic. Their business framework was able to absorb the shocks that the pandemic brought.

As the pandemic hit, some organizations were able to start their digital journey earlier than others. Companies that were already concentrating on technical improvements before the pandemic, for example, were able to address issues like moving their employees to a work-from-home arrangement.

On the other hand, companies using outdated systems had a tough time transitioning to a digitally supported system. Several companies shut down permanently due to outdated processes and technologies and having no plan to address them. Their technology was not compatible enough to allow employees to work or do other day-to-day tasks remotely, resulting in implementation delays and operational interruptions.

These companies eventually had to go through a recovery phase, highlighting the importance of a long-term and robust digitalization strategy. In addition, strategic leaders were also more prominent during this period thanks to plans previously put in place before the pandemic. The use of the pandemic's "learned lessons" is critical for future planning and development.

Regarding the importance of strategic leadership at all levels and having a culture of growth and innovation:

"The fact is, culture eats strategy for lunch. You can have a good strategy in place, but if you don't have the culture and the enabling systems … the [negative] culture of the organization will defeat the strategy."

—Dick Clark

With the increasing competition in the business world, companies need professional and visionary leaders who can empower, train, and encourage people to carry out strategic actions to ensure the company's progress in the long run.

One important aspect to recognize when ensuring that the company's operation aligns with its strategies is that people at all levels of the organization have to understand its primary goal. At every level, workers seek guidance and insight from their leaders about what the future will be like and how they can contribute to its success.

Therefore, leaders must improve their productivity by concentrating on strategic tasks to respond to competing demands and identify opportunities hidden among the pile of problems. Each position, department, and individual must comply with the company's primary goal and contribute to it. Therefore, it is necessary for each leader on every level of the organization to formulate and incorporate their own unique, independent approach that is in sync with the organization's goal and lead their employees accordingly. This culture and environment encourage employees to use their skills, align their efforts with the organization's goals, and contribute to its success.

To harvest strategic opportunities or navigate the risks ahead, strategies within the organization require constant analysis. There must also be discussion on new developments, transformations, and reinventions in the services, activities, procedures, and mindsets.

When there is strategic leadership at all levels, sustained success is inevitable. The right leadership team will recognize when it is time for a change and ensure organizational health by making the necessary adjustments.

Organizational Health and the Need to Change

To maintain a healthy body and proactively address areas that could be considered risk factors, I visit my doctor regularly. When I am in her office getting a physical, she generally checks five key areas to determine how healthy I am: my blood pressure, pulse, bloodwork, reflexes, and temperature. I will submit to you that our organizations are the same way. While leaders consider many factors when focusing on areas of change, I believe these are the five most critical to monitor regularly:

1. Customer Satisfaction (CSAT) (blood pressure) – How delighted are your customers?
2. Revenue (temperature) – Are you experiencing an increase or decrease in income? What is the cause?
3. Culture (pulse) – What are the shared values, attitudes, and behaviors that define your company?
4. Retention (reflexes) – What is the turnover rate for your employees?
5. Results (bloodwork) – How often do you achieve the goals you set out to accomplish? Do you reach your KPIs consistently?

If these five areas are in the desired range, it is a good indication that your organization is healthy. However, because each measurement can affect the others, *it is critical to design and implement an action plan and then track the outcomes if any of these vital areas begin to exhibit a negative trend.*

Here is the cadence I recommend for effective monitoring that will inform priorities:

1. Customer Satisfaction – Weekly
2. Revenue – Weekly
3. Culture – Quarterly
4. Retention – Monthly
5. Results – Weekly

You will learn how to address any concerns and measure the health of your organization in later chapters.

Personal Reflection

If you were in a leadership capacity during the COVID-19 pandemic, take some time this week to reflect on what you learned as a leader. If you were not in a leadership position at this time, do some internet study on the subject. Make a list of five things you can do to improve your strategic leadership skills.

Chapter 2

Expose Your Next Level

"Creating the next level of results requires the next level of thinking."
Rory Vaden

You have maxed out how far you can take your team, department, or company if you ever get to a point where you feel like you have maxed out your skills. There is always a next level, and I remember the first time I realized this truth. I had been working at a White Castle restaurant as a manager for several years. One day, I came home from a sixteen-hour shift that I was mandated to work because the second-shift manager had called off again. I walked into the house, took off my hat, my hairnet, my Shoes For Crews, my shirt with the logo, and my black khakis. I glanced at the floor and found all the tiny particles of onions that had dried up in my shoes' slip-resistant bottom and scattered all over my carpet. The smell of onion rings, sliders, cheese sticks, French fries, and chicken rings permeated the atmosphere and my hair. I knew at that moment I wanted a different career. While there is absolutely nothing wrong with working in the fast-food industry, I knew that coming home smelling like food every day, not being challenged in my work, and wearing a uniform was not my destiny. Although I knew there was something more for me, I had no idea what "more" was.

When all my background up to that stage was in the restaurant business, how would I switch careers? I knew that if I was trying to reveal or expose the next level, I had to open myself up to new knowledge and ideas. I started spending time with people who had the type of careers that interested me. This exposure created an interest in the tech industry, so that is what I pursued.

From the back of an industrial kitchen to taking on the industry's toughest challenges in the boardroom, the need to do better still exists. Many years and countless achievements later, there is still a next level for me.

I seemed to go through the same process throughout my career any time I felt like I needed to develop in a particular area:

1. Vocalize the desire for next-level results
2. Visualize what next-level results look like
3. Value the outcome enough to act
4. Validate the steps necessary to get there
5. Vigorously pursue next-level results

Every great leader cyclically goes through the above process to develop both personally and professionally. You cannot take your team to the next level if you haven't identified the next level. Likewise, you can't identify the next level for your organization or department's vision of success if you haven't exposed the next level for yourself.

It's essential to be a strong leader and manager. There is always another level to everything, including your leadership. Leadership is about getting people to appreciate and invest in your mission. Working with and managing your team to accomplish your goals is all about maintenance and seeing that things happen as they should every day. Both are necessary, but only leadership will take you to the next level.[4]

No matter how successful you are, you can always explore another level, discover new things, make mistakes, improve yourself, experience failures, and develop game-changing ideas. You will have a higher chance of learning more unique concepts and having new ideas if you expose yourself to new people and new information. As a result, you will create an appetite for more growth, expose your next level, and then act towards achieving it.

The Differences Between Managers and Leaders

Leaders	Managers
Agents of change	Resistant to change
See the end from the beginning	See the past and now
Focused on the people	Focused on the process
More focused on why	More focused on how

Big-picture perspective	Snapshot perspective
Uncover opportunities	Uncover obstacles
Cast their vision by explaining the strategy	Carry out the vision by breaking it into steps
Challenge the status quo	Embrace the status quo
Motivated by long-term objectives	Motivated by day-to-day objectives

If you dive into history and search for successful leaders, you will see that each one of them was never afraid of exploring things and experiencing failure. That is because they knew that the only way to boost their brains with new ideas was to let go of the fear of the unknown and try out something unorthodox. Not only does this provide insight towards what they are searching for, but it also increases knowledge and understanding. As a leader, you might have a particular set of skills and expertise, but you will explore a whole new range of possibilities as you step into new territory. These possibilities will polish your skills and knowledge, which will help you excel!

> "The manager administers; the leader innovates. The manager has a short-range view; the leader has a long-range perspective. The manager asks how and when; the leader asks what and why. The manager has his eye on the bottom line; the leader has his eye on the horizon. The manager accepts the status quo; the leader challenges it."
> —Warren G. Bennis

The quality of your leadership is determined by the quality of the questions you ask yourself daily. These questions allow you to explore possibilities, fail forward, and challenge yourself to change. Exploration equips you with the necessary information and confidence to become a more decisive leader, allowing you to better influence your team.

Suppose you want to develop as a leader. In that case, you must have the confidence to handle change, chaos, and discomfort so that you can transform your organization's culture into one that practices purposeful strategies and tactics to scale your team and the entire organization for the future shocks mentioned earlier.

You must have confidence as a leader.

"Experience tells you what to do; confidence allows you to do it."

—Stan Smith

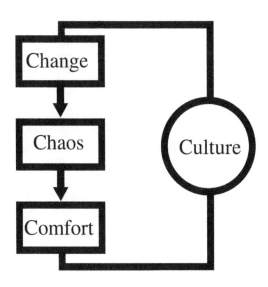

The culture of your organization or department is mainly dependent on how the leaders handle change, chaos, and discomfort. Here is the ongoing process that occurs in thriving businesses:

1. The leader introduces changes to future-proof the organization or department.
2. Those changes disrupt the culture and cause uncertainty and chaos amongst managers and within departments.
3. After the staff has accepted the changes, those changes become the new norm and everyone gets comfortable again.
4. The culture changes for better or for worse depending on the confidence and courage of the leaders.

Several years ago, a company I was working for as the head of the services and support department acquired another company. My responsibility was to draft, implement, and operationalize the plan for merging the support team and customers from the other organization with our processes. This was no small feat. Because of the new products and the complexity introduced with the acquisition, our procedures needed to change to accommodate our new responsibilities. This caused a disruption with everyone involved because each group did things the way they had always done them and felt there was no need to change. As a result, there was resistance initially, along with apprehension to follow the new process. It took about a year to get to a place where we were "comfortable" again. After this experience, our culture got stronger because we were able to identify rising leaders who stepped up during the process. We also continually measured progress, met with the team to measure success, and gave necessary input on adjustments. Although this was an uncertain time, I believe leadership confidence made the difference. We cast a vision, explained why, kept the team informed, and they gave their buy-in on future changes.

When people look up to a leader for guidance, a leader needs to have the faith to lead them and provide the advice they need. This is even more important in uncertain situations.

This faith is the confidence that a leader has about their ability, capacity, skills, and knowledge to handle any problematic situation that arises. The confident behavior of a leader has a massive impact on their team's function and overall success. So how do you measure your confidence as a leader? Use my Four Cs Confidence Test to determine your leadership capacity and identify your next-level leaders who can navigate your team through this process.

The Four Cs of Leadership Confidence Test

Answer the four questions below using a 1–5 scale: 1 being less likely or not well and 5 being highly likely or very well.

Circle the number that best represents you, with 1 being the less likely or not well and 5 being the highest:

1. How well do you handle organizational changes?

1   2   3   4   5

2. How well do you handle organizational chaos?

    1   2   3   4   5

3. How often do you step outside of your comfort zone?

    1   2   3   4   5

4. How often do you intentionally take action to promote a healthy organizational culture?

    1   2   3   4   5

Then total your score:

- **1–8:** It is important that you find ways to intentionally step outside of your comfort zone, address conflicts/chaos quickly, promote an inclusive culture, and be open to change to demonstrate your confidence as a leader during transition. Confident leaders are aware of their strengths and blind spots and are not afraid to seek assistance as needed. They are not frightened by the strengths of others but rather focus on their own strengths while leveraging the group's skills. Having a peer network or support group is a useful way to discuss common, actual concerns. It will reassure you that "I'm not the only one who feels like this."

- **9–15:** Which area(s) did you score the lowest? Maybe you like new changes, but you don't want to adjust your processes because you are comfortable doing what you've been doing. Or maybe you spend so much time addressing chaos and conflict that you don't spend time working on your team culture. Regardless of your greatest opportunity area, it is important that you find ways to intentionally address them to demonstrate your confidence as a leader during transition. Even if you're a little nervous on the inside, you can always "fake it till you make it" by acting confident. Also, if you feel you do not have the experience necessary to lead through this change, consider connecting with a mentor who is strong in the areas you'd like to develop in. A leader's self-awareness will improve as a result of feedback. Furthermore, leaders who solicit input are regarded as more confident than those who do not.

- **16–20:** While this score is an indicator that you feel confident to lead through the upcoming changes, it is important to remain self-aware. Knowing your leadership strengths will boost your confidence, and acknowledging your development gaps will help you figure out where you need to improve. A leader that is emotionally intelligent has self-confidence. Be sure to remain humble and foster an environment of inclusivity. When one of your coworkers or colleagues achieves a goal or does something fantastic, tell them and everyone else about it. This isn't about brag-worthy accomplishments; it's about cultivating the habit of seeking out and appreciating others' achievements for a more cohesive team.

After you complete this assessment for yourself, measure your peers. If your scores don't indicate that you are ready to handle the changes necessary to get you to the next level, don't be too concerned. Several strategies in later chapters will help you identify the best next step as it pertains to your people strategy and making sure your leaders are equipped.

Being confident is good for the team you lead, the business's success, and your well-being. Confidence makes you less prone to stress. It gives you the power to control the negativity and panic that emerges under challenging situations.

Leaders are supposed to have a vision—a clear goal that determines where they want to go and how to lead their people. But what does it take to reach those goals? To have a vision and inspire people to follow you? It requires confidence. Confidence in yourself and the knowledge and skills that you have. The confidence to be able to "take your shoes off" and do things a new way and explore new possibilities. Unless a leader is confident enough to do so, he cannot have a clear idea about where he wants to go and strategize the plans for his team accordingly.

Experience tells you what to do, while confidence provides you with the courage to go for it and face all kinds of situations. Learning and having knowledge about things in advance helps a leader feel more confident about the decision. Having knowledge and understanding of the field and the factors that can influence their decision helps leaders see things from several perspectives. It assures them that they have gone through all the possible factors that can impact their choices and reduced the risk factors beforehand.

A confident leader can sort things out when a problematic situation arises by analyzing the problem with their knowledge and experience. Confidence keeps the others calm and focused on solving the issue rather than panicking. Experience, skills, and knowledge make a leader aware of the possible risks in order to devise a plan to tackle potential situations.

Learning and gaining knowledge can be a daunting experience. When we are learning, there comes a time when we feel less confident about being able to do specific tasks. But that's one of the steps towards learning. We fail again and again before we can master our skills. And all the failed attempts are no loss either. Those failures add to our knowledge. When you face difficulty and failures, combine your experiences with the knowledge.

Often, we fail to connect what we have learned in theory and practice. But when we combine what we know with what we have experienced, it develops into confidence as we see and experience the results ourselves, good or bad. And that allows us to find different ways to tackle the situation or do things more efficiently—a quality that every leader must have.

A leader's confidence in trying new things in the workplace can have a positive impact on the team. It can help create an environment, training, and procedures that allow the staff to learn how to manage work and develop new ideas in a new system. It reinforces their confidence in working in ever-changing business environments.

Reinforcing confidence in teams is very important when an organization goes through changes. The change can be abrupt or slow, but it is common for employees to resist the change.

A leader must provide employees with encouragement, knowledge, and training to help the employees embrace changes in such situations. This way, resistance is minimized.

When leaders present themselves confidently and provide their employees with ways to adopt changes, employees feel more prepared. As a result, the employees will be more confident with the change and the new system. In the next chapter, we will discuss developmental strategies and how you can grow as a leader through exposure to help develop and scale your organization.

> *The quality of your leadership is determined by the quality of the questions you ask yourself daily.*

Personal Reflection

To expose your next level, you must ask yourself thought-provoking questions:

- Am I a leader or a manager? What made me answer the way I did?
- Why do I think that exposure to new ideas is necessary for growth?
- How do I handle failure? How do I handle success?
- What is something I had exposure to recently that changed my perspective?
- What have I learned about myself in the past sixty days?
- What is one thing that I wish I had known when I began my career?

- What are three life principles that are necessary to get to the next level?
- What does the next level look like for me?
- What is stopping me from getting to the next level? How will I overcome it?

Chapter 3

Expose Yourself to New Ideas

*"Everyone's perspective of themselves and others
is based on the limitations of their exposure."*
Kamala Harris

E xposure to new environments and situations has a lot to do with growth. Sometimes exposure is unintentional and we experience it whether we want to or not. Yet, intentional learning is more critical for the development of a leader. This means it is necessary for leaders to knowingly introduce themselves to diverse situations and conditions, learn new things, and polish their abilities.[5]

Leaders Need Exposure to Learn and Grow

Why is that so important? In my career so far, I have seen how the business world goes through various shifts. Some of those changes are caused by external variables, and some by the internal climate of the organization. For a leader, it is necessary to remain one step ahead of all changes. The leader must know what steps to take to adjust to those changes and lead their team accordingly.

There are inevitable shifts. You can find major corporations throughout history struggling because their executives did not know how to cope with changes. The leaders struggled to respond to changing trends, triggering the collapse of the organization. A leader must prepare and have the skills needed to improve their organization in order to escape a demise. How can leaders prepare themselves for such situations? The answer is simple: exposure. They need to know how things work in a particular context to learn new things, bring up their game, and make adaptive plans for potential shifts in the future. To learn how various environments act, however, a leader must first introduce themselves to these environments. Other executives from the same or separate sectors, novel developments in the business world's external and internal climate, consumers, colleagues, and other external influences will make these exposures inevitable. This will open the leader up to new and improved strategies and better outcomes as a byproduct.[6] Here are the steps you should take to get exposed to fresh ideas:

1. Read books specific to your opportunity areas.
2. Read articles and blogs specific to your industry to stay current with trends and industry standards.

3. Listen to podcasts specific to your industry.
4. Complete training and courses related to development gaps. Visit our website for available courses: https://www.xposeyoursolutions.com.
5. Hire an executive coach/mentor. Visit our website to learn more about our coaching services: https://www.xposeyoursolutions.com.
6. Join a mastermind group for accountability and to leverage solutions.
7. Network with peers from other industries to benchmark.
8. Ask the people closest to you for candid advice on ways you can improve personally and professionally. This will help you overcome blind spots.

Strategic exposure helps a leader understand and apply certain things to their actual situation in advance. This gives them the leverage to know and predict things in advance while improving their capacity to implement improvements in their business. Success depends on how capable a person is at dealing with and responding to changes in today's age. Today, leaders must conquer other realms, unlike in the old days where individuals gained achievement by merely mastering their domains. People had enough information back then to do their work, nothing more. All they had to do was become skilled at one job and step up the ladder. Today, if a boss tries to do this, their business is going to collapse. They won't be able to contribute value to their business. The world we know today is different than what it was.

Rapid, constant, and disruptive changes now require leaders to change and develop. It involves exposure to diversity in many aspects. That's why, as leaders, we must discover the correct solutions by strategically opening ourselves up to creativity, new concepts, and fresh possibilities.

We have to upgrade our information pool continually. Leaders must improve themselves and continually learn new things to deal with the latest and ever-changing market conditions. Think of this progression and growth as your well-being. To see how your body is doing, you need regular checkups. As you age, your body experiences change. The constant change in your body requires you to take proper medication, change your diet, and exercise differently.

To improve your fitness, you must understand what your body wants and make improvements accordingly. It is essential to make the necessary improvements before your current routine causes harm. But how do you know what you need to do to protect your health? Informational exposure. The checkups you get done expose you to new data, helping you find the areas to address. The same happens when it comes to the development and growth of a leader. It would be best to expose yourself to new solutions and ideas to determine what you lack and what changes are required.

It takes ownership and accountability to accept that you cannot go on with the same amount of data you had. If you want to succeed, it takes a deliberate commitment to establish yourself as a leader.

Let me share my experience here. During my career, I worked as the head of a services and support department. I got the opportunity to lead through several acquisitions. We absorbed the personnel, procedures, clients, and corporate systems of those businesses. While challenging, we operationalized the changes to ensure our customers were delighted.

During the first acquisition, I initially did not know how to cope. However, being in a position where I had to lead the change, I decided to expose myself to new information. I started researching how to integrate my department, interviewed the acquired company's staff, and consulted with other stakeholders. I also had a mentor who had the experience of leading through an acquisition. I went to see him and even inquired about his experience. Via his input about leading through acquisition, I got a lot of data. This supported me in formulating a strategy.

I managed to ensure our customers did not notice or experience a decline in service. In fact, despite the significant changes, there was ultimately an improvement in the service provided to the customers. We also extended the range of products supported by our team, increased our net promoter score (NPS) and CSAT ratings, enhanced efficiency, and strengthened staff involvement. All of this happened because I strategically exposed myself to new information by acknowledging that I did not know everything. I accepted that I did not have all the answers.

A leader must not hesitate to admit that they do not know everything. There is nothing wrong with asking questions. Your leadership level is measured more by the quality of the questions you ask than by the quality of the responses you give. Leaders should expand their networks just like I did. It helped me learn new things. I was able to ask my mentors, other leaders, and employees for help. My success as a leader was possible because

I had a solid network to help me learn new things and integrate them into my department.

Exposure helps you see your weaknesses and strengths. Just as a business performs a strength, weakness, opportunity, and threat (SWOT) analysis to identify gaps and scale their growth, I believe you must complete a SWOT analysis on yourself to identify gaps in your development so that you can address them and scale your growth.[7] Doing this helps me stay forward-thinking in my actions. Understanding your strengths, weaknesses, opportunities, and threats enables you to create a game plan to get to the next level. After completing this analysis, you have a better understanding of where you stand and what you must do to reach your goal. You can do your SWOT analysis below. You will have a clearer sense of the best plan of action when you know your starting point.

Strengths	Weaknesses
What do you do well?	What internal flaw(s) hinders you?

Opportunities	Threats
What are the internal factors within your control that could change you for the better?	What are the external factors outside of your control that could hinder you?

Now that you have completed your SWOT analysis, do the following:

1. Identify opportunity areas that would have the most significant impact and act on them.
2. Use your strengths to take advantage of opportunities.
3. Address weaknesses and minimize threats by capitalizing on opportunities and operating in your strengths.

You must broaden your perspective based on the work you have done and experienced.

When your organization is going through changes of any size, you will have to develop and change yourself accordingly. If you remain the same way, you will not lead the organization through a different phase. Unless you intentionally put yourself in situations that push you to grow, you cannot direct the employees.

EXPOSEYOUR™ Assessment and Development Plan

As mentioned, I believe every great leader must have a development plan, and you can start with a personal SWOT analysis. Once you have that sorted out, you can start on your development plan.

I have developed a framework through which you can assess your leadership capacity. It addresses the nine core competencies that great leaders must have to navigate change in their organization and lead their team to the next level. It is called EXPOSEYOUR™.

> "Good leaders have experience. Great leaders have exposure."
>
> —Shara Hutchinson

There are distinct levels of leadership, just as restaurants have various levels. Typically, restaurants are rated according to stars. If you are at a five-star restaurant, for instance, and ask the server where the restroom is, they will escort you to the door. If you're at a restaurant on a lower scale and ask the same question, they're more than likely going to point and tell you to find it for yourself. The distinction is that one showed the way, and the other suggested the way. Only suggesting the way can trigger confusion and delay, while demonstrating the way saves time and builds trust. Great leaders are like servers at five-star restaurants. They lead the way through EXPOSEYOUR™.

EXPOSEYOUR™ is an acronym in which each letter identifies a leadership capacity required to advance the company to the next level:

- **E**xecutive presence – The capacity to project courage and sobriety under pressure.
- **P**urpose – The capacity to understand the motivation behind an initiative and the determination to follow through on the actions required to attain the desired outcome.
- **O**ptimization – The capacity to utilize staff and resources efficiently and effectively.
- **S**trategy – The capacity to develop, implement, and operationalize a plan to scale your business, team, or department.
- **E**xecution – The capacity to identify the best next move, execute the strategic plan through actionable steps, and monitor accountability outcomes.
- **Y**ourself – The capacity to be you, recognize your abilities, deliver to your full potential, and respect the talents of others to work collaboratively.

- **O**pen-mindedness – The capacity to remain receptive to new ideas, challenge the status quo, and disagree respectfully.
- **U**ncertainty – The capacity to recognize areas of inexperience, ask the right questions, see possibilities despite complicated conditions, and successfully lead through transformation.
- **R**esponsibility – The capacity to operate with integrity, be reliable, and take ownership regardless of who is at fault.

Keep in mind that when we speak about leadership capability, it goes beyond your growth. It encompasses your entire leadership team and all staff. Exposure to new information and establishing a culture of learning helps to incorporate all skills and knowledge to deal with the changes in practical settings of business. Leaders are not simply advisors recruited to improve the personal and technical talents of individuals. For the individuals for whom they lead and work, they must build an authentic learning and evolving environment. EXPOSEYOUR™ is an ongoing process. You must keep improving with the requisite changes to inspire the people you lead, get to the next level, and guarantee that your organization will last long-term.

Personal Reflection

Based on the definitions above, how would you rate your EXPOSEYOUR™ leadership capacity? How would you rate your leadership team? Rate all leaders and average your scores to calculate the score for your organization.

☆☆☆☆☆ Never
★☆☆☆☆ Occasionally
★★☆☆☆ Sometimes
★★★☆☆ Often
★★★★☆ Most of the time
★★★★★ Always

Use a scale of 1–5 to rate yourself as well as others.

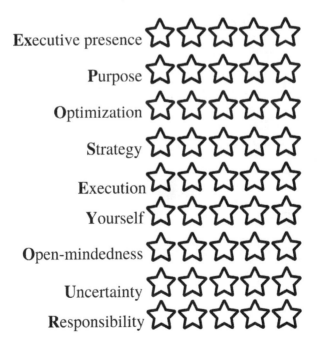

Executive presence ☆☆☆☆☆
Purpose ☆☆☆☆☆
Optimization ☆☆☆☆☆
Strategy ☆☆☆☆☆
Execution ☆☆☆☆☆
Yourself ☆☆☆☆☆
Open-mindedness ☆☆☆☆☆
Uncertainty ☆☆☆☆☆
Responsibility ☆☆☆☆☆

Are you a five-star leader? Is your leadership team considered five-star? If not, how many stars do you have? Use these results to assist with formulating professional development plans to get you and your staff closer to becoming five-star leaders so that you have the potential to scale up with your company.

Phase 2

Take Your Shoes Off

Chapter 4

The Employee Experience

"None of us is as smart as all of us."
Ken Blanchard

or all visitors, my parents have a rule: no shoes in the house. Therefore, when anyone visits, including me, we are required to take our shoes off. Guests are frequently caught by surprise the first time they enter and see the "take your shoes off at the door" sign. Thoughts like, *Are my socks clean? Do my socks match?* oh, and of course, *Are my feet presentable?* race through their heads. It truly takes vulnerability to take your shoes off, so the only people who come over are those who do not mind the policy. My parents never pay a lot of attention to their visitors' feet, however. Their main concern is keeping their floors clean by not tracking in debris from outside.

As an innovative leader, you must enact a similar policy for the boardroom, or wherever you conduct meetings: no shoes allowed. If you're going to enact change, you must create a safe space in which to share new ideas, encouraging others to leave outside "debris," or pre-existing beliefs about running your organization, at the door. This will require vulnerability.

In the previous chapter, I addressed the importance of personal growth. Now that you understand how you can start working on yourself and improve yourself as a leader, let's turn to your team's development.

> "If you want to go fast, go alone. If you want to go far, go together."
>
> —African Proverb

Significant results within your organization require a team effort, making it necessary also to develop your team. That's because, as a leader, you need to prepare yourself to prepare others—your team.

You cannot walk the road to success without having a team, no matter how clever, creative, talented, inspired, and enthusiastic you are. Similarly, you have to develop and inspire the team to appreciate and collaborate on a common objective. I feel it is a lot more complicated to develop a team than it is to develop yourself. That is because under your guidance you are going to have a dynamic team with varying abilities and drivers. Much as a parent with several children must react differently to empower them, a leader must observe and understand with whom they are working to unleash their unique gifts. But why is having a winning team so important?

Well, I can answer that question for you with two questions:

1. Will you be able to carry out all the action items from your business strategy alone?
2. Will you be able to achieve the desired business results alone?

If you answered no to both questions, I know two things about you:

1. You have a great vision.
2. You will need the right team to bring your vision to fruition.

I like symphonies. One thing that amazes me is how each musician or performer can project different sounds and notes, yet the sound produced is magical and blends as if from one instrument. This is what it is like when you have a winning team. Everyone plays their part, delivering a magnificent outcome.

It sounds challenging, and it is. But like your own development plan, you can lay out a plan to understand the gaps in your team and start working on filling those gaps. You can spur your team members to work together towards a common goal. When you're successful, the outcome is engaged, high-performing employees.

The world's greatest leaders and managers give their employees a safe space to fail and share their thoughts.

Before we get into the discussion of the whats and hows, you must understand that this is more than just having a short talk with your employees or team members. You must start by knowing your team members to coach them to success. It requires understanding their personalities, work styles, strengths, weaknesses, needs, and wants. When it comes down to all these, question yourself. How much do you know about your team members other than their names and their job titles?

A Strong and Diverse Team is Critical to Success

A diverse group is becoming a business necessity instead of an ethical banner that companies hold to show their commitment to embracing and valuing difference and change.

Whether they bring new cultural, ethnic, or national backgrounds or new skills and knowledge, people from various backgrounds are brought together in a team to offer fresh ideas and creativity to the organization. This type of culture promotes a healthy learning environment in which people may learn from one another and foster innovation.

How? Different people have different perspectives, and based on their knowledge and skills, each can analyze the risk factors by weighing other possibilities. In a pool of diverse skills and knowledge, there is a higher chance of detecting upcoming problems to create a sustainable business plan that can help the business survive through difficult times and seize the opportunities that come with it.

The People

One of my first jobs was being a manager at a fast-food restaurant. I must say, this experience equipped me for leadership. I learned how to serve. As a store manager, I was responsible for profit and loss (P&L), inventory, shift management, speed of service, escalations, and overall customer satisfaction. In addition, I helped with cleaning, sweeping, mopping, and cooking the food for customer orders. While some managers would sit in the office most of their shift doing paperwork, I stayed out on the floor as much as possible to work with the team. Every staff member felt valued and would go out of their way to work on their day off if I needed additional assistance. I believe this was because I modeled a leadership style that communicated value to every employee. Just because I was the manager, I was not more important than the cashier or the person stocking inventory. We were all on the same team with different roles that were all important. As director, senior director, and CEO, I carried this mentality with me throughout my career and into my own business. *All employees matter, and they need to know it!*

> *The world's greatest leaders and managers make all employees at every level feel valued.*

The People Strategy

As leaders, we have an inspiring vision, a comprehensive and strategic plan, and we know the results we want to achieve. However, we often overlook the necessity to develop a strategy for the most important asset: the people who will ultimately make it happen.

Does your organization have a people strategy? How do you plan to achieve your organizational goals through your employees? When I work with organizations, all have a business strategy, but I rarely see a people strategy. When I ask the organization's leading figures about it, I usually get a blank look in return. Yet, when discussing their employees, they all agree that their people are the most critical asset.

For any business optimizing its workforce, it is crucial to develop, grow, and improve performance. This means that the leaders require a good business strategy and an effective people strategy to make their business goal achievable. You cannot overlook the importance of aligning your business goals with an effective people strategy. Some may think that employees can align themselves to the business goals by themselves. But keep in mind that the details and plan needed to do so are not usually in place.

Remember that a human resource (HR) strategy is not a people strategy. There is a vast difference between both. HR strategy is for its human capital to align with the organization's activities. It includes focusing on development, pay and compensation, performance, recruitment, and onboarding. However, a people strategy focuses on outlining the organization's relationship with its workforce.

Align Your Business Strategy with Your People Strategy

If your corporation hopes to achieve your desired market objectives, you must choose an organizational model that helps implement your business plan. A host of issues occur when the structure and strategy of an organization are in contrast with each other.

In my experience, I've found that top corporations purposely choose the layout of their organization, maintaining consistency with their policy. Yet, often executives do not understand best practices with the organizational model. Because of this information gap, they select a system at odds with their corporate philosophy, encouraging leaders to let the structure evolve rather than proactively change it to scale for where they are going. As a result, they make poor hiring, firing, and structural decisions and end up in a hierarchy that doesn't meet their needs—resulting in employee dissatisfaction and mismanaged resources.

I remember working with a nonprofit organization that was having issues with turnover. New employees were resigning within thirty days, and the executive director was feeling burned out. After assessing all employees using the PI Behavioral Assessment and the PI Employee Experience Survey, I was able to determine the following:

- The staff felt like they had competing priorities because they were without the appropriate resources to manage their workload.
- The staff felt like they did not receive recognition for their achievements.
- The mission and overall strategy had changed to focus more on community outreach rather than legislative work.
- The executive director had been in the same position for twelve years and did not want to change his focus from the legislative work.
- The team was very process-driven, introverted, and uncomfortable with change.

After gathering this information, I worked with the executive director and the board and determined that their organization was not structured to support their business strategy. They took immediate action and did the following:

- They created a job profile that identified the personality traits needed for the open position that they could not keep occupied. They initially searched for people similar to the current staff, but they wanted a more social person for community outreach efforts.

- They initiated an employee recognition program and added a "kudos" segment to the agenda of their weekly meetings to allow time to recognize staff when warranted.
- The acting executive director decided to be repositioned to the executive assistant in order to focus on policy work. He assisted the board in interviewing and hiring a new executive director to lead the organization to its next level by focusing on the new strategic direction: community outreach.
- They scheduled time to update their strategic plan to include the new community outreach direction.

Within six months they were fully staffed, their retention improved, they operationalized their new strategic plan, and they re-engaged employees. Often organizations make the error of forming teams and divisions around an employees' skill set. However, this can create complications for future growth. If the individual leaves the organization, it would be impossible to fill the role because the job requirements depended on an individual's talents and shortcomings and not on the need.

Restructuring a department sometimes makes sense, even if it means that a senior executive is no longer a rank higher than other subordinates. In the end, you must do what is best for the team. When you do, the outcome is rewarding. The world's most outstanding leaders and managers don't just ask if they have the right strategy and the right people; they also ask if they have the proper structure.

Why Is a People Strategy Important?

Today, employees are not just an asset—they are the most important asset. They are the investors of their time, energy, and talent. They need to get something out of their efforts; something meaningful and fulfilling. So if you do not include them as a vital aspect of your business strategy, they will find someplace that does.

If you want to ensure that your business strategy is sustainable, you have to keep employees as an integral part of business growth. It would help if you shaped your plans to meet the needs of your employees by understanding that a business's ability to retain the right people in the right places is the most critical competitive advantage.

Think of people strategy as the logical extension of an organization's business strategy. It is a blueprint that tells leaders how to utilize their company's talent to deliver on their primary objectives. People strategy is not subservient to the business strategy. If used the right way, it helps the leaders decide the best approach to reach their goals.

It is doubtful that local organizations or start-ups will have their corporate plan well established. The ethos of these companies represents the founder's ideals, strategy, and beliefs of a leader. Nevertheless, as the business starts expanding, the control stretches over different territories. Then the leaders must articulate the culture through standards and value statements. When the corporation grows, new workers move into the organization with distinct approaches from diverse backgrounds. As a small business, you do not need to worry as hard about a plan for individuals. But if you have a large talent pool and want your organization to expand more, you will need a plan for people to enforce an organizational culture built to survive shifts and changes.

It would be best if you had a clear idea of what your organization needs. Does the organization need to be innovative, or is it focused on systemized processes? Understanding the key objectives will help you figure out the skills you will need in your teams. Do your goals require the team to be good at fundamental research and innovation or good at exploiting developed ideas? These questions will get you the answers that support your goals: whether you need to focus on the existing talent and polish your employee's skills or need to explore new talent.

There is no single or right way to develop a people strategy. That's because every organization has a unique business strategy, structure, culture, and workforce. To create the best people strategy, leaders need to consider multiple factors. And for that, leaders must engage in understanding their employees and be involved with their development.

The following are considerations for devising a people strategy. These considerations are crucial for intentionally leading your employees strategically for growth and scalability:

- **The company's mission**
  As a leader, you must explain the organization's mission and vision to your team members. Allow any decisions you make to come out of these statements. Whenever there is confusion about whether to implement an initiative, ask if it lines up with the company's core values. If it does not, the obvious response is "do not proceed."
- **The company's objectives**

It is impossible to make it to a destination you've never been to before without directions. Communicate objectives to staff with milestones and timelines to ensure results.

- **Business strategy**

  The business strategy explains how you will achieve your objectives. When you share the strategy, your team has a blueprint for their actions and feels more confident with changes.

- **Corporate capability**

  While devising a people strategy, you should weigh the capabilities that exist in the company. Think about how you can utilize them now and in the future.

- **The people resources**

  Think about the measures that define the talent and skills of the people at the individual and team levels. What determines the talent resources in your company?

Just like any strategy, the people strategy needs to be reviewed and adjusted over time. It is vital to ensure that your plan is still relevant to the organization and its environment by considering internal and external changes. Suppose you want this process to become an intrinsic part of the organization's strategy development. In that case, you will have to make sure that people strategy informs the organization's overall strategy.

The Employee Journey

Everything an employee learns, does, sees, and feels is part of the employee experience, from the minute they glance at your career website until the moment they leave your business. The employee journey is a framework used by HR to analyze and improve the employee experience by combining all of the employee's experiences over their tenure with the company.

There are five stages:

- Stage #1: Recruitment
- Stage #2: Onboarding
- Stage #3: Development
- Stage #4: Retention
- Stage #5: Exit

Within each of these stages are moments that determine whether that employee will stay or leave. These major or small moments all contribute to the employee's experience, and they provide chances to listen to their needs, be more equitable and inclusive, and bridge the gaps that exist.

If you want to enhance employee satisfaction, you can sketch out the journey your employees take while working for your company. By graphically mapping the different processes and emotional states that workers experience when interacting with the company, businesses may prioritize resources and financing, define responsibilities, and pinpoint crucial moments that matter.[8]

Just as you can segment customers by their persona to provide an individualized journey, as we will talk about in the next chapter, you can do the same thing for your employees. Understanding the personas of each of your staff members will give you the insight necessary to increase engagement and retain top talent.

The Employee Experience Matters

An organization's environment plays a huge role in team development. A healthy organizational environment drives business growth by attracting its employees and addressing their needs and functions. It is essential to foster a safe environment for employees to share their thoughts and survey them to handle employee experience matters.

> "A leader is best when people barely know he exists . . . when his work is done, his aim fulfilled, they will say: we did it ourselves."
>
> —Lao Tzu

For example, a creative member of your team may want the freedom to express themselves. In that case, please provide them with a working environment that gives them that freedom. Similarly, career-driven people may wish for opportunities to prove themselves to climb the corporate ladder. Analytical employees may want to have a job that requires them to solve problems. Even though all your employees have different needs, they have one leader: you.

Find out what matters most to the team members, what they are good at, and how to accomplish corporate goals by leveraging their creativity. Always inspire them. Find out what truly motivates them. Generate incentives to fulfill their needs. Helping the team members to engage in their position in the company is the secret to growth. In addition to all the advice, introduce them to the complexities of business opportunities. Offer them the ability, under your guidance, to use the skills they learn as they grow. Giving them chances to exercise their talents demonstrates that managers value them.

Moreover, the whole process will help you recognize the gaps in your team. As a leader, you can help them strengthen weaker skills and bring them to a higher level of performance that complements their roles in the organization. Preparing your team this way will help you build a knowledgeable and skilled workforce that can also work independently without having a leader micromanage them.

Measuring the Employee Experience

To maintain a positive employee experience, I recommend doing the following:

- Conduct quarterly employee engagement surveys, address issues that arise, measure improvement, and provide updates to staff.
- Hire an outside agency to conduct an annual, anonymous employee satisfaction survey. Assemble your leadership team to discuss the results, address any critical areas, measure results, and provide updates to staff.
- Create clear job descriptions, career path opportunities, and guidelines for promotions. Provide a professional development plan for any employee who desires to advance within the organization. Hold all managers accountable for integrating these conversations into their regular check-ins.
- Conduct exit interviews when employees leave to uncover trends and issues to address.

- Allow employees to conduct self-reviews to promote healthy dialogue with their direct manager around performance.
- Measure and track employee turnover. Act as needed.

Chapter 5

The Customer Experience

I f you hadn't noticed, I intentionally positioned this chapter after the chapter about the employee experience. This is because if your employees are not happy, they will not create a delightful experience for your second most important asset: your customers.

For any business, customers are important stakeholders. Everything from planning to the execution of a product or service is about satisfying the end-users. Over time, the preferences and choices of end-users change, so a business must innovate its customer services along with other business innovations.

As Jerry Gregoire puts it: "The customer experience is the next competitive battleground."

And a battleground it is.

Customer service is what retains a client, making them choose that company or brand over others. Unless a business knows what its customers expect next, how is it supposed to devise strategies to meet those needs?

The future of the customer experience and the future of your business are intimately intertwined. If your customers are not happy, they will not be customers for long. As a result, you won't be in business for long. There is a continual variation in what clients want and expect. Companies need to continually discover new ways to serve consumers and improve customer loyalty to remain ahead of the competition. Ultimately, companies that do not conform to delivering a higher level of customer service endanger their future.

Have you ever dated someone and they seemed like the perfect mate, only to find out a few months or years down the road that they were not who you thought they were? If you feel betrayed and sever the relationship, you do not engage with that person again, and you don't refer anyone else to date them. Sometimes organizations sell potential clients a dream and then shatter their hopes by breaking their expectations or failing to keep up with the demands of the industry. Either way, this triggers a decline in renewals and referrals, which jeopardizes future growth.

In *The Rules of Woo: An Entrepreneur's Guide to Capturing the Hearts & Minds of Today's Customers* by Cindy Solomon, there is an excerpt from a story that I believe illustrates how many companies handle prospects as opposed to how they treat their customers. I've paraphrased the story here:

A man dies and finds himself at the pearly gates. The guard at the gate is holding a clipboard, checking in people as they arrive. The guard looks up and smiles as he sees the new gentleman in line. He says, "You are so lucky that you died today! There's a special we're offering today only!"

"Really?" says the man.

"Yeah, you get to choose whether you want to go to Heaven or Hell."

The man asks, "How will I know which to choose?"

The guard quickly responds, "Not to worry! We let you stay a day in each place so you can make an informed decision about where you want to spend all eternity."

The man says, "Okay. I think I'd like to go to Hell first."

The guard smiles and motions him into an elevator directly behind him. "Great! Down you go!"

The doors open up onto a white sandy beach. People are playing in the surf, drinking drinks with little umbrellas, and dancing to a calypso band. It's absolutely . . . well, Heaven! The man spends an enjoyable day, comes back up, steps out of the elevator, and says, "That was wonderful! I can't wait to see what Heaven is like!"

Back into the elevator and up he goes! The doors open to white fluffy clouds, harp music, and lots of smiling, happy people. It's very nice but not really very exciting. After his day, the man goes back down in the elevator and says to the guard, "I can't believe I am going to say this, but . . . I'd like to go to Hell please." The guard says no problem, and on the man goes.

This time, when the doors open, instead of seeing the beach and hearing the calypso band, he's greeted by people running and screaming, fire, and brimstone. He stands there dumb-founded. The devil comes up to him and barks, "What's your problem? Get in here!"

The man responds, stuttering, "There must be some mistake! I was here yesterday! There was a beach and drinks with little umbrellas! What happened?!"

The devil responds, "We get this all the time. Yesterday, you were a prospect. Today, you're a customer!"[9]

When this happens to your clients, there's no guarantee that they'll be with you for a long time. Therefore, to recognize the value of achieving what is promised, it is crucial to look through the customers' eyes. Innovation becomes the core factor in ensuring that the client's experience is strong enough to keep them and increase trust with them.

A business market is never free of competition. Therefore, it is imperative to build trust and continually discover newer ways to serve consumers and improve customer loyalty to remain competitive. Ultimately, companies who do not conform to delivering a higher level of customer service endanger their future, and firms who stay up-to-date reap the benefits. To sum it all up, an above-average customer experience is as important as any other aspect of maintaining growth.

Why the Customer Experience Matters in Innovation and Sustainability

As mentioned before, a business cannot survive without customers. In the previous chapters, I said it is vital to focus on business and the ever-changing external environment to experience long-term success. The aim of the whole structure of a company and its strategies is to grow and plant its roots within the market, considering and evaluating all the typical challenges ahead.

Like many different factors, customer needs are continually changing. The products and services you are offering may be what the customers expect now. However, it may not be for long. Times and trends will change, and these very customers will likely expect and need something else. To meet these changing needs and demands, you must be innovative. This innovation should not only be for the current customers, but also for potential customers if you want your business to excel in the future.

A business needs to think like an innovator—always coming up with ideas to improve their services and products or to introduce something new in the market. A business should be able to see the market changes coming from a distance. Predicting future demand by analyzing the current market pattern can provide a company with solutions even before the customers realize they are expecting something else.

The bottom line is: customer service aims to keep customers happy. Nonetheless, even if a company keeps its customers comfortable temporarily, it must constantly revise its strategies regarding the overall customer experience. There are many ways to do so depending on the nature of the business and its products and services. You see, any business can take over their competitors and make their way to the top by harnessing power from the latest technologies and using forward thinking. Here are a few points to help you understand this:

1. Customers want to buy from an innovative business

Research shows that innovation drives purchases and enhances the company's image for customers. Innovation is compelling. It causes people to buy products without fully comprehending their use or relevance to their life. Most customers buy products that make them appear innovative in front of others. Furthermore, with the changes happening and new technologies emerging within the market, people like to buy things that complement other innovations.

2. Customers want to be the first

Many customers purchase first-generation products. Some people want to buy things that are new to the market. Current customers might expect new and innovative products from you, but they also promote your products and attract potential customers for you.

3. Customers pay a premium for innovation

Innovation in customer service makes customers pay more for unique products and services. If you offer consumers the innovation they seek, they will pay the premium knowing that they are not getting the same product elsewhere. It increases the worth of your product much more than any substitute in the market.

4. Invent, reinvent, and listen to the customer

For any business, coming up with new ideas for products and services is the most crucial driver of innovation. In this digital age, it has become easier to listen to and understand the needs of the customer. Today, innovation is driven by businesses listening to their current and potential customers and understanding and responding to their needs. Based on the information gathered, companies make changes, continue to improve current products, and produce new ones.

Here are a few examples of companies that future-proofed their business by innovating their customer service:[10]

1. **Tim Hortons' gamification of their loyalty program**
   Tim Hortons, Canada, upgraded their customer reward offerings. They added new gamification elements to the app that help them track their customers' reward progress and build a way to make customers visit their coffee shop frequently. Customers participate in games to earn prizes while leveling up for more benefits.

2. **Nike provides fast service for busy shoppers**
   Nike has never been behind when it comes to customer experiences. But knowing the need for continual innovation and that there are changing customer demands, Nike has taken things to the next level. Their Speed Shop provides a convenient way for online shoppers to try on the products they order online in stores. They introduced a special entrance for customers that can be used and

unlocked via smartphone to find their shoe locker. They can try on their shoes in the store without interacting with a person and check out on their smartphones.

3. **Mercedes' AR owner's manual**

   Car manuals can be very bulky, and that makes customers dread reading them. To solve this problem, Mercedes came up with the idea to develop an app that serves the purpose. This new app provides a useful and convenient replacement for the bulky manual and tracks everything about the car and its driver. The app, Mercedes Me, showcases the features of the car to the user without the hassle of reading a manual. Moreover, it provides the user access to data regarding the vehicle from anywhere in the world.

With Social Media, Organizations Cannot Hide if They Provide Poor Service

Today, purchases are driven by social media platforms, blogs, and websites. Customers themselves are driving this purchasing process by using these channels. But it does not just stop there. The influence of these channels goes far beyond just the purchases. Once the products start selling, customers use these platforms to review the services and products, impacting the company's reputation.

That's why it has become necessary for businesses to adopt new technologies and approaches to digitize their customer service and measure the overall customer experience. It's critical to let customers know you value feedback. The kind of customer service that a company provides becomes transparent through these channels. If a company fails to deliver what it promises, it cannot stay hidden.

With easy access to information, customers have more choices when it comes to making purchases. Customers are using social media platforms and different channels to connect with other customers while sharing their experiences. Such connectivity impacts a customer's purchasing behavior. Given the high cost of winning new customers, it has become essential to ensure your customers remain loyal to you. And not just in the present, but in the future as well.

To build customer loyalty under such circumstances, companies must upgrade their frequent contact points with customers. This way, they can review their plans and people and align them to meet the changing demands. Moreover, companies need to focus on innovation that promotes the best possible customer experience.

Delighting Your Customers

To delight your customers, I believe you must provide a PROPER customer experience. I came up with this acronym as an easy way to remember how to stand out and create loyal customers who are raving fans.

Here is what a PROPER customer experience usually does:

- **P**ersonalize communications – When possible, don't use automatically generated responses or bots. Sometimes, knowing a human being is responding means the world and mitigates miscommunications. If you must use an automatically generated response, be sure to include when your customer can expect a response in your email template.

- **R**ead and respond to customer feedback – In all of my roles, including my business, I read all customer feedback or have someone else review it. Any negative feedback warrants reaching out to the customer for a resolution. Customers are so surprised when someone from my team contacts them.

- **O**verdeliver – *Always* give more than what is expected. Creating a "wow" moment for the customer can make a big difference in their loyalty.[11]

- **P**rovide multiple channels of communication – I've noticed that many companies are moving their support models to prioritize self-service channels. While self-service and email options are effective, having various contact methods such as chat, phone calls, and video tutorials makes you more accessible. Rather than guiding the customer away from direct contact, give them an option to make a choice.

- **E**ngage in real-time support – In today's fast-paced world, customers do not want to wait. Every moment wasted provided an opportunity to choose a more responsive vendor.

- **R**esolve issues – When a large percentage of customers make a complaint about a service or product, that's enough proof to promote changes. When you resolve problems based on their feedback, customers know they are heard and are more likely to stick around long-term.[12]

When I was the director of service and support at a software company, we maintained an average CSAT score of above 97 percent and an NPS score of above 85 consistently. Our customers were so delighted with the support we provided that many joked, saying, "I wish you were the IT department at our organization." Our team provided 24/7 live support for phone calls, tickets, and emails. We did not have automatically generated email replies, but rather someone from our team looked at each ticket and gave a customized statement to indicate that we had investigated the issue. This allowed us to catch the high-priority problems more quickly and resolve them faster.

In addition, we did not have targeted call handling times to give agents as much time as needed to assist the customer without competing with a buzzer. Our KPIs were selected to drive exceptional service. Responses and ratings from our surveys showed that what we were doing worked. Either the manager or I would directly read, review, and respond to negative customer feedback. When the client received a call to resolve issues along with a follow-up to check on the resolution, they were surprised. I believe that measuring the customer experience and adjusting as needed contributed to providing PROPER service and delighting our customers.

> "Make a customer, not a sale."
>
> —Katherine Barchetti

Tracking the Customer Journey

A competitive strategy to make and keep your customers requires a leader to interact with different teams to work in a specific direction to obtain a collective outcome: a positive customer experience. If you have a good team and strategic leadership but don't prioritize your customers, it will stunt your growth.

Your teams can use customer journeys to map and track their complaints and strategize the area of improvement needed to boost sales. The awareness, consideration, and decision-making stages of sales help you envision how customers pass through and encourage each interaction.

The customer journey is a step-by-step process that any prospect takes to become a customer. The customer's experience along this whole journey is far more important than the pricing or product for company success. Therefore, a leader needs to know how to map out and track a customer's journey to provide an excellent user experience.

The customer's journey is not measured or tracked in miles, but instead in experiences and interaction with the company. Any interaction stimulates the potential customer through the sales channel, and when you get it right throughout the journey, you gain customer loyalty. Their journey begins through sales conversations, social media posts, website visits, blog articles, search queries, or customer support calls.

As I said, every customer is different. There are no similar customer journeys, but every potential customer moves through the same stages, which are:[13]

- **Awareness**

  The customer knows they have a problem and starts searching for a solution.

- **Consideration**
  The buyer or potential customer does research and starts to understand their needs and gain more information.
- **Decision**
  Having a deeper understanding of what they want or need, the buyer or potential customer selects a solution that best fits them.
- **Customer loyalty**
  Having consistent positive experiences with a business, the buyer/customer becomes a regular customer and an advocate of the brand.

Once the customer purchases and becomes loyal to your brand, you must continue to track their journey, matching your communication strategies with customer expectations at each stage by measuring their overall experience.

Customer Relationship Management

A huge component of making the customer journey delight-ful and promoting customer loyalty is intentionally managing customer relationships. This involves assigning relationship managers or customer success professionals to understand industry and customer needs and track them in a customer relationship management (CRM) software to recommend products and services. They also proactively address issues that may impact the customer's experience. The objective is to strengthen customer service relationships, encourage client retention, and increase sales. CRM systems collect data from customers across many points of contact with the business, such as the company's website, phone calls, live chat, direct mail, marketing materials, and social media.[14] Providing customers with a dedicated advocate also helps champion changes within the organization on their behalf.

As a part of one of the roles I held in the past, I was a customer success manager as our department worked to operationalize a true customer success function. During this time, I managed several customers who were identified as high-risk based on our customer health reports. I tracked their overall satisfaction based on criteria I had previously identified in the customer health requirements and implemented a specific communication plan based on their unique situation. Each interaction and next steps were tracked in a CRM software.

Example Account Communication Plans

- Watchlist
- At Risk
- Critical Care
- Custom

Example Communication Plan Actions

- Highlight Customer Update in Leadership Meetings
- Weekly Meeting With Internal Account Team
- Weekly or Bi-Weekly Status Report Call with Customer
- Weekly Status Report Emailed to Executive Team

Example Customer Tactics

	Communication Plan Actions			
Account Communication Plans	1	2	3	4
Watchlist	N/A	N/A	N/A	x
At Risk	N/A	Monthly	As Needed	x
Critical Care	x	Weekly	x	x
Custom	x	As Needed	As Needed	x

You can use the example communication plans, actions, and tactics above to categorize your customers and then track interactions using CRM software. Below are some reasons why you may want to use a CRM.

CRM systems may help companies of all sizes, from small businesses to large corporations, by offering:[18]

- Customer information, such as previous purchases and interaction history, which might aid customer care agents in providing better and faster service.
- Reporting and visualization tools so organizations may uncover patterns and insights about their consumers by collecting and accessing customer data.
- Automation for menial but necessary sales funnel and customer care duties.

Example CRMs

These are in no particular order. If you decide to go with a particular platform, I recommend drafting the requirements for your business, conducting your own research, and choosing the one that addresses your needs.

- Hubspot CRM
- Insightly
- Keap
- Monday.com
- Salesforce
- Zendesk
- Zoho CRN

Measure the Customer Experience

It is important to measure customer satisfaction if you want to improve the value of the customer experience. How can something like consumer service be calculated when it appears very qualitative and includes many business elements? There are far too many explanations for an empty shopping cart or failure in retaining a customer. Even in the business world, where you can observe and track the customer's journey from start to end, it can be challenging to identify the exact problem.

Merely asking customers if they liked their buying experience doesn't work to get lucid explanations. When a purchase goes without a glitch, no one wants to complete a lengthy survey, which might compromise results.

You need a holistic approach to measuring the customer's experience. There are many methods to do so. Below are some metrics that businesses use to get a more precise, overall picture:[16]

Metric 1: Customer Satisfaction

The customer satisfaction metric or CSAT is where most organizations are focused. There are two parts:

- **Explicit CSAT**
  In this method, surveys and questionnaires are sent to customers. These questionnaires can be placed on the official shopping websites or at the end of online checkouts regarding the shopping experience.
- **Implicit CSAT**
  The Implicit method includes product review ratings, mystery shopping scores, timeliness delivery statistics, etc. This approach seeks to highlight the facets that might get overlooked via indirect customer satisfaction questionnaires.

Metric 2: Customer Loyalty and Retention

Customers who have a great experience are more likely to return or renew than customers with a poor experience. To measure loyalty and retention, focus on metrics like:

- Net promoter score (NPS)
- Repeat orders and renewal rates
- Purchase frequency and average order size
- Upsell ratio
- Participation rates in your loyalty programs
- Customer engagement score

Metric 3: Advocacy

Observe if your customers recommend your goods and brand and endorse them. This is an essential means of determining if you are providing a good customer experience. You can do it by monitoring:

- Price sensitivity: Do price changes impact your sales?
- Sentiment scores and trust ratings: Are customers willing to go out of the way to support your product or service?
- Event participation: How much do your customers get involved in your brand?

Metric 4: Quality and Operations

When a service or product does not fulfill expectations, customers will develop concerns that will turn into doubts if you refuse to address them. Data reveals that after just two bad experiences, 42 percent of customers switch from a company. Hence, quality is essential from the beginning to the end to ensure a good customer experience.

Tie In the Employee Experience with the Customer Experience

As much as I have focused on and emphasized the importance of prioritizing customers in a company's success, I cannot neglect that employees and teams are among the most critical assets in this process. Studies on customer experience suggest that the principal competitive differentiator for any company is improving every aspect of the customer process instead of concentrating on enhancing the overall customer experience. This includes producing highly engaged employees.

Data reveals that businesses with exemplary customer service have 1.5 times more engaged employees than companies with lower satisfaction. Moreover, businesses with highly engaged employees perform 147 percent better than their competitors.

In short, happy employees equal satisfied customers and vice versa. Ensuring higher engagement and connections with employees means employees are more passionate about their jobs. Moreover, satisfied customers can play an important role in improved employee engagement. Highlighting good customer interactions can offer employees value and purpose and can create motivation and productivity positively.[17]

Improving the Customer Experience

To improve the customer experience, I recommend doing the following:

- Measure and track NPS for customer engagements. Act on feedback as needed.
- Measure and track CSAT for customer interactions. Act on feedback as needed.
- Measure and track overall customer health by the various categories in your industry. Act on feedback as needed.
- Measure and track renewal or repurchase ratio. Adjust as needed.
- Measure and track customer engagement—meaning how much are they using your products or services. Adjust offerings as needed.

Note: Use the methods that are most relevant to your industry. The most crucial point to remember when improving the customer experience is something I call following the STAR:

1. **S**core – Use metrics and key performance indicators to take a snapshot of the customer sentiment.
2. **T**rack – Monitor these metrics over some time.
3. **A**djust – Make changes to your service offerings, products, or even metrics as needed.
4. **R**epeat – Start the process over again after changes have been made to measure impact.

Chapter 6

The BAREFOOT Method™

*"If you can't solve a problem,
it's because you're playing by the rules."*
Paul Arden

From the earliest stages of our lives, we are told and taught to follow the rules and norms. To some extent, these rules are helpful to maintain discipline and achieve success. However, to lead a life where solely those rules and standards drive your actions can tamper with your true potential.

As we get older, the conditioning of our minds further conforms our behavior to our surroundings, and thus we begin living in "autopilot" mode. Let me prove it to you. Have you ever driven somewhere, only to arrive at your destination and wonder how you got there? Have you ever performed a task the same way for so long that you no longer had to think about how to do it because it happened automatically? If you answered yes to either of these questions, the same holds true for you. You have been conditioned in some area. In the past, I have driven all the way to the office, arrived, and then wondered how I was able to stop at the stop signs, drive at the appropriate speed, and exit at the appropriate ramp without paying attention. When I think about it, it is kind of scary to know that I could operate an almost three-thousand-pound vehicle and not remember any detail from the trip.

I read an interesting article a while back that provided an explanation to the phenomenon that drivers are the most likely to crash at locations closest to their homes because "drivers are less attentive and aware when they're driving on familiar roads." The author said, "Studies have consistently shown that when we're not actively paying attention, we may fail to perceive things that are right before our eyes in a phenomenon known as 'inattention blindness.' When driving down a familiar street, we may be more likely to drive on 'autopilot' without our full attention, increasing the odds that we miss important information, such as construction warnings or a new street sign."[22] Therefore, I conclude that no matter how familiar you are with a route, it is imperative to challenge your comfort zone to avoid calamity. The same principle applies to leadership.

Every organization has its predetermined path, better known as best practices and processes. If you are determined to succeed, you must be committed to a culture of innovation and constantly challenge the "this is how we've always done it" mindset. You must be bold enough to stand barefoot in the boardroom.

Yes, it can be a little scary to be a rebel; to take your shoes off when everyone else has theirs on. I know it can be comforting to color inside the lines and never take any organizational risks. However, where there is little to no risk, there is little to no reward. The familiar path will get you the familiar result. Then the familiar result will cause your business or department to experience a CRASH simply because you missed an important detail or failed to make a necessary turn. And no one wants to experience an organizational CRASH because this could lead to a total loss.

- **C**ustomer dissatisfaction
- **R**evenue loss
- **A**wful culture
- **S**taff turnover
- **H**indered results

If you are experiencing a CRASH—a negative outcome in any of the areas mentioned above—and desire to lead your team through change successfully, let us walk through how to avoid an unnecessary loss in your business.

The BAREFOOT Method™ I practice comprises proven leadership steps that will empower you to seize every opportunity to make things better, challenge the familiar paths, and take the necessary risks to prepare your team along the way.

BAREFOOT Method™

The BAREFOOT Method™ that I introduce in this chapter is an acronym of eight letters. It comprises proven strategies and tactics that I have implemented to achieve exceptional results and the framework I've observed while watching other successful leaders and mentors. Each word of this acronym explains a step to effectively lead your team through change and demonstrate the heroic measures that the world's greatest leaders utilize to reach the next level or reach their BHAG.

Have you ever heard of the term "BHAG," coined by Jim Collins and Jerry Porras in their book *Built to Last: Successful Habits of Visionary Companies*? BHAG is an acronym for a "Big Hairy Audacious Goal"—a vision for your company's next ten-to twenty-five years of growth that pushes it to new heights. This massive target should be both terrifying and exhilarating, and it should guide your path in three-to-five-year chunks.[23] Does your company have one? If not, please read *Built to Last* before jumping into the BAREFOOT Method™. If so, read it anyway.

Note: Think of your BHAG as your long-term vision and the BAREFOOT Method™ as a navigation tool to get there.

The Prerequisite

Chapter One of *Built to Last* discusses the significance of knowing your company's Hedgehog concept to determine your BHAG. I am revisiting this topic because to utilize the BAREFOOT Method™, you must have a "why." It would be best if you had something audacious to look forward to, a reason to "stand on the table with no shoes"—an exciting goal; a BHAG aligned with your company's passion.

Here are a few BHAG examples taken from an article I read:[24]

- Become the most recognized and respected consumer brand in the world (Starbucks)
- Every book ever printed, in any language, all available in less than sixty seconds (Amazon)
- A computer on every desk in every home (Microsoft)
- Land a man on the moon and return him safely to earth (1960s America)
- Leaders and organizations around the world certified as BAREFOOT change management leaders and using the EXPOSEYOUR™ leadership capacity model (Xposeyour).

Step 1 – Write Your BHAG

Now that you have seen a few examples, write out your BHAG. Schedule a brainstorming session with the leadership team to discuss your ten- to twenty-five-year vision. Here are questions to consider for your discussion:[25]

- In your wildest dreams, what would you like to accomplish? Describe what the company will look like when it is operating at a level that achieves that success.
- What is the benefit for your customers, your employees, your shareholders? Paint the mental picture for yourself and your team.
- What is one clear, compelling, and measurable goal that will be reached when the vision becomes a reality? Make a list of potential ideas.

- Which of these ideas seems to convey the feeling and spirit of the vision? Narrow your list down to two or three potential BHAGs.

Step 2 – Test Your BHAG

Now that you have brainstormed some ideas for your BHAG, you can determine if it aligns with your passion by answering all of the following questions. If the answer to all eight questions is yes, you have a great BHAG and are ready for the BAREFOOT Method™. If any of the answers are no, continue brainstorming until it meets the criteria.

Use these BHAG test questions from Jim Collins' Vision Framework:[26]

1. Do you find this BHAG exciting?
2. Is the BHAG clear, compelling, and easy to grasp?
3. Does this BHAG somehow connect to the core purpose?
4. Will this BHAG be exciting to a broad base of people in the organization, not just those with executive responsibility?
5. It is undeniably a big hairy audacious goal and not a verbose, hard-to-understand, convoluted, impossible-to-remember mission or vision statement?
6. Do you believe the organization has less than a 100 percent chance of achieving the BHAG (a 50–70 percent chance is ideal), yet at the same time believe the organization can achieve the BHAG if fully committed?
7. Will achieving the BHAG require a quantum step in the capabilities and characteristics of the organization?

8. In twenty-five years, will you be able to tell if you have achieved the BHAG?

The BAREFOOT Method™ Overview

Before using the BAREFOOT Method™, here are a few guidelines to consider for achieving the desired result:

1. This framework does not have to be followed sequentially. It is important you gauge where you are as an organization and act accordingly. Your leadership team should be equipped by this point to navigate effectively.

2. You can only eat an elephant one bite at a time, so do not try to change everything at once. This process takes at least a year to work through, so enjoy the quick wins along the way and be patient for the long-term victories.

3. As the former heavyweight boxing champion, Mike Tyson, so eloquently said, "Everybody has a plan until they get punched in the face." This means even the most well-thought-out plans will be faced with unexpected events. Following the STAR (score, track, adjust, repeat) rule as mentioned in the previous chapter will allow your organization to course-correct and quickly bounce back from any challenge.

4. Real organizational transformation must take place at the top first. Therefore, it is imperative to have executive sponsorship to experience real change and lasting results.

5. This framework begins with the assumption that you have a strategic plan, BHAG vision, and mission in place.

B – Break

Corporate transformation may be difficult to achieve, as many businesses are learning. Why? Because we frequently fail to verify whether our organization's norms, or the invisible factors that govern people's behavior, are supportive of the new path we are attempting to create. Therefore, the very first stage of the process is to "break." The objective is to understand your organizational norms, recognize areas that need to be addressed, and intentionally break patterns that deviate from the desired outcome.

How to Break the Organizational Norms

Breaking organizational norms must be done with extreme caution because exposing the unwritten rules can lead to uncertainty and emotional pain, which most employees and leaders would rather avoid. When leaders collaborate with others to establish and express the organization's vision, they show bravery by ensuring that everyone is on the same page.

Step 1 – Expose Norms by Interviewing Employees

Interview as many employees as possible and thoroughly document their responses. Let the employees know the leadership team is embarking on some initiatives to make improvements to the company and culture and you need candid feedback to know what areas to address. Here are sample questions you can ask. Feel free to add any of your own.

1. Do you believe employees are promoted because of seniority or performance? Why?

2. What are the traits that make up the top performers in the company?
3. If you were training a new employee, what would you tell them to watch out for as it pertains to culture or best practice?
4. Is it acceptable to make a mistake? Why or why not?
5. Are problems addressed or ignored? Why do you feel this way?
6. What is one thing we could do as an organization that would drastically change business for the better?
7. Do you feel comfortable being honest about issues? Why or why not?
8. What is the biggest issue being faced by our organization today?

Notes:

-   Do not be surprised if the feedback is different than your perception. Many times leaders are not aware of the unspoken rules that guide employee behavior.
-   You can also put these questions in an anonymous survey form, distribute it to employees, and capture the responses that way.
-   However you decide to distribute the questions, be sure to explain the "why" to employees.

Step 2 – Investigate Norms by Charting Responses

1. Group feedback responses by common themes and aggregate totals to chart trends.

2. Create a word cloud for the top three words used for each question.

3. Create a word cloud for the top thirty-five to fifty words used in the feedback.

4. If your company performs exit interviews with employees upon their departure, review feedback for the past year to observe common themes.

5. Draft a summary of findings and present it to the leadership team with recommendations to address major concerns.

Note: You should perform this same analysis in six months to a year to track any changes.

Step 3 – Break Norms with The 1L3R Rule

1. **L**ead the change you want to see – For example, if employees believe that asking for help demonstrates ineptitude but you want to foster greater cooperation, purposefully ask for help in meetings as a leader to model the behavior you want to see. You may also organize team-building exercises to emphasize everyone's efforts.

2. **R**emove obstacles to progress – For example, if employee feedback indicates that most of the weekly meetings they attend are meaningless and a waste of time, you may implement a company-wide meeting framework that involves rating meeting effectiveness at the conclusion and then aiming to maintain a particular score as a business.

3. **R**eward the desired behavior – For example, if feedback revealed employees feel they are valued more because

of seniority than performance, implement a performance-based incentive system to recognize individuals and/or teams for their achievements.

4. **R**einforce the change – Observe employee behavior on a regular basis and, if needed, change the determinants of behavior using performance metrics, leadership role-modeling, or organizational policy. You will build a dedicated, inventive, high-performance culture and achieve a competitive edge by baking these changes into everyday actions and providing accountability.

Breaking the rules/norms on purpose can aid you in developing techniques and practices that will guarantee your company is moving in the correct path, ensuring its long-term viability.

A – Assess

Assessments are necessary for a business to examine and analyze where it is today and where it wants to go in the future. The objective of analyzing your current condition is to discover deficiencies and determine how to address them. This stage provides the groundwork for future organizational changes and the metrics that will be used to assess their effectiveness. You will take three assessments:

1. Organizational Health Assessment
2. Overall Operations Assessment
3. Barefoot Impact Assessment

Remember when we talked about organizational health metrics in Chapter 1? I shared that when I have my annual physical to assess my overall health, my doctor generally checks five key areas: blood pressure, pulse, bloodwork, reflexes, and temperature. As mentioned, your organization is a living, breathing organism that also has five critical areas to monitor:

1. Customer satisfaction (blood pressure) – How delighted are your customers?
2. Revenue (temperature) – Are you experiencing an increase or decrease in revenue? What is the cause?
3. Culture (pulse) – What are the shared values, attitudes, and behaviors that define your company?
4. Retention (reflexes) – What is the turnover rate for your employees?
5. Results (bloodwork) – How often do you achieve the goals you set out to accomplish? Do you reach your KPIs consistently?

If these five categories are within the acceptable range, your company is in good shape. When your objective is sustainability, however, more in-depth assessments are required to build a more thorough action plan. Therefore, during the assessing stage, your team will examine all areas of your business, including where it is now and what you can do to make your firm stand out. The areas covered in the overall operations assessment are as follows:

- People
- Processes
- Purpose

- Priorities

Finally, you must establish your capacity by assessing the amount of influence the projects you are working on will have on the business. This will allow you to make the required modifications. This assessment is called the Barefoot Impact.

Note: Completing these assessments should stimulate discussions among your leadership. As you design your objectives, you will discover areas that may need to be addressed for your efforts to succeed.

Step 1 – Organizational Health Assessment

1. Compare your customer satisfaction score for the previous year or the most recent quarter completed to the original target set for that same time period. Did you reach your target? Did you have a target?

2. Compare your revenue for the previous year or the most recent quarter completed to the original target set for that same time period. Did you reach your target? Did you have a target?

3. Compare your employee engagement survey for the previous year or the most recent quarter completed to the original target set for that same time period. Did you reach your target? Did you have a target?

4. Compare your retention/turnover for the previous year or the most recent quarter completed to the original target set for that same time period. Did you reach your target? Did you have a target?

5. Compare the percentage of completion of the high-level corporate goals for the previous year or the most recent quarter completed to the original target set for that same time period. Did you reach your target? Did you have a target?

6. Use the below chart to fill in your responses and calculate your performance health score as follows. See the example for additional details.

    If you reached the target in that area, mark the grade as 100 percent. If you did not reach the target in an area, mark the grade as 50 percent. If you did not have a target/goal set for that area, mark the grade as 25 percent. Once you have all your scores entered, calculate the average. That result is your organizational health score. A score of 90 percent and above indicates a healthy organization.

Calculate Your Organizational Health Score

Category	Score
Customer Satisfaction	
Revenue	
Retention/Turnover	
Employee Engagement	
Goal Completion	
Health Score	

Example

Category	Score
Customer Satisfaction	100
Revenue	50
Retention/Turnover	100
Employee Engagement	25
Goal Completion	100
Health Score	75%

*In the example above, the company has a moderate health score and they achieved their customer satisfaction, retention, and goal completion objectives. They did not, however, reach the revenue target, and there was no benchmark against which to evaluate employee engagement. This revealed the possible need for a metric to assess employee happiness as well as a deeper investigation into the cause of the revenue target failure.

Step 2 – Overall Operations Assessment

The goal of this assessment is to identify areas that could be potential blind spots for your company. Take note of the areas you answer no to when you respond Yes (100) or No (50) to each question. These are the areas where you should concentrate your operational planning efforts.

For each statement, score your business as 100 percent if the answer is yes and as 50 percent if the answer is no. The average of all those scores will give you an overall operations assessment score. Once you have all your scores entered, calculate the average. That result is your overall operations score. A score of 95 percent and above indicates a healthy overall operation.

Question	Score
	100 for Yes & 50 for No
People	
Everyone is committed to the vision and enjoys working together.	
We have the right leadership team to take us to the next level.	
Everyone has goals that are in line with our strategic plan and they are held accountable for their individual contribution through performance reviews.	
All staff members are in the best position for their skill set.	
All managers in the company meet with their direct reports regularly to set goals, track progress, and work of professional development.	
Processes	
All company meetings have a clear agenda, start and end on time, and are followed up with emails that detail the next steps.	
All fundamental procedures are documented, current, and easily accessible to anyone who requires them.	
We have a budget and are monitoring it regularly and adjusting behaviors as needed.	
We have a system in place for updating procedures so that they are always up-to-date.	

We have a system in place to collect regular customer feedback, keep track of satisfaction levels, and respond appropriately.	
Purpose	
All staff members understand and can recite our company core values and/or vision statement.	
We have a well-documented and communicated company vision and mission statement.	
We have defined messaging guidelines that everyone follows when expressing our value proposition to clients and prospects.	
Our target market is well-defined, and our sales and marketing activities reflect this.	
Employees believe that what we do as a company is meaningful and they are dedicated to the company's mission.	
Priorities	
We have a defined three- to five-year strategic plan that we are working towards.	
Everyone has goals that are aligned with our strategic plan and they are held accountable for their results in their performance evaluations.	
We have an internal project management team or someone responsible for managing internal projects.	
In order to stay on track, all teams identify, analyze, and resolve critical issues that affect priorities on a regular basis.	

We have a specific change management plan in place to guarantee effective communication with employees and plan implementation.	
Performance Score	

Example

Question	Score
People	
Everyone is committed to the vision and enjoys working together.	100
We have the right leadership team to take us to the next level.	100
Everyone has goals that are in line with our strategic plan and they are held accountable for their individual contribution through performance reviews.	100
All staff members are in the best position for their skill set.	100
All managers in the company meet with their direct reports regularly to set goals, track progress, and work of professional development.	100
Processes	
All company meetings have a clear agenda, start and end on time, and are followed up with emails that detail next steps.	50
All fundamental procedures are documented, current, and easily accessible to anyone who requires them.	50

We have a budget and are monitoring it regularly and adjusting behaviors as needed.	100
We have a system in place for updating procedures so that they are always up-to-date.	100
We have a system in place to collect regular customer feedback, keep track of satisfaction levels, and respond appropriately.	100
Purpose	
All staff members understand and can recite our company core values and/or vision statement.	100
We have a well-documented and communicated company vision and mission statement.	100
We have defined messaging guidelines that everyone follows when expressing our value proposition to clients and prospects.	100
Our target market is well-defined and our sales and marketing activities reflect this.	100
Employees believe that what we do as a company is meaningful and they are dedicated to the company's mission.	100
Priorities	
We have a defined three- to five-year strategic plan that we are working towards.	100
Everyone has goals that are aligned with our strategic plan and they are held accountable for their results in their performance evaluations.	100

We have an internal project management team or someone responsible for managing internal projects.	100
In order to stay on track, all teams identify, analyze, and resolve critical issues that affect priorities on a regular basis.	100
We have a specific change management plan in place to guarantee effective communication with employees and plan implementation.	100
Operational Score	95%

*The company in the preceding example has an excellent overall operating score. They did, however, recognize that to function more effectively, they needed to enhance their process documentation and meeting structure.

Step 3 – Barefoot Impact Assessment

The Barefoot Impact Score runs from 1 to 5, and the results will give you an idea of how the change will affect your company's day-to-day operations. Many executives take on major initiatives without first analyzing their impact, resulting in overworked staff who fail to fulfill their objectives. After you have determined the projected impact, you'll be able to respond and assess risk.

Please respond to the following ten questions. Choose the one that best describes your circumstance. Then, in the table below, enter the number linked with the question. For instance, if you select "Department" as the answer to the question, "Who is impacted?," you would write "3" in the box next to that question on the table. To calculate your Barefoot Impact, take the average of those ten scores once you have entered all your answers.

Note: The score of 1 indicates a low impact, while a 5 indicates high impact.

- Who is impacted?
  1. Individual
  2. Group
  3. Department
  4. Division
  5. Everyone
- How many are impacted?
  1. <20
  2. 20–150
  3. 150–500
  4. 500–1000
  5. <1000
- Process Impact
  1. Nothing Changing
  2. Little Change
  3. Some Change
  4. Significant Change
  5. Everything Changing
- Technological Impact
  1. Nothing Changing
  2. Little Change
  3. Some Change
  4. Significant Change
  5. Everything Changing

- Is there a necessity for organizational restructuring? (i.e., organizational chart, job descriptions, etc.)
  1. Nothing Changing
  2. Little Change
  3. Some Change
  4. Significant Change
  5. Everything Changing
- Do you currently have a culture that celebrates risk-taking?
  1. Risk-Taking Encouraged At All Levels
  2. Risk-Taking Encouraged In Certain Departments Only
  3. Risk-Taking Encouraged For Leaders Only
  4. Risk-Taking Encouraged For Some Individuals Only
  5. Risk-Taking Not Encouraged
- How long will it take to implement the changes?
  1. <1 month
  2. <1–3 months
  3. 3–6 months
  4. 6–12 months
  5. >12 months
- Will employee compensation or benefits be impacted by the changes? (i.e., layoffs, demotions, promotions, change in out-of-pocket expenses for benefits, etc.)
  1. No Impact
  2. Little Impact
  3. Moderate Impact
  4. Significant Impact
  5. Major Impact

- Is this the organization's first time going through a change of this magnitude?
  1. We Have Successfully Implemented Multiple Changes Greater Than This Magnitude
  2. We Have Successfully Implemented Multiple Changes Similar To This Magnitude
  3. We Have Successfully Implemented Multiple Changes, But Not Of This Magnitude
  4. We Have Successfully Implemented Smaller Changes
  5. We Have Never Implemented A Change
- Do you have dedicated change managers and project managers for this initiative?
  1. We Have Both
  2. We Have Either A Project Manager or Change Manager
  3. We Have Both But They Have Competing Priorities
  4. We Do Not Currently Have Either But Plan To
  5. We Do Not Currently Have Either And Do Not Plan To

Barefoot Impact Answers

	Actual Score
Who is Impacted?	
How many are impacted?	
Process Impact	
Technological Impact	

Is there a necessity for organizational restructuring? (i.e. organization chart, job descriptions, etc.)	
Do you currently have a culture that celebrates risk-taking?	
How long will it take to implement the changes?	
Will employee compensation or benefits be impacted by the changes? (i.e. layoffs, demotions, promotions, change in out-of-pocket expenses for benefits, etc.)	
Is this the organization's first time going through a change of this magnitude?	
Do you have dedicated change managers and project managers for this initiative?	
Barefoot Impact	Average Score

Example

	Actual Score
Who is Impacted?	3
How many are impacted?	2
Process Impact	2
Technological Impact	1
Is there a necessity for organizational restructuring? (i.e. organization chart, job descriptions, etc.)	3

Do you currently have a culture that celebrates risk-taking?	2
How long will it take to implement the changes?	2
Will employee compensation or benefits be impacted by the changes? (i.e. layoffs, demotions, promotions, change in out-of-pocket expenses for benefits, etc.)	5
Is this the organization's first time going through a change of this magnitude?	5
Do you have dedicated change managers and project managers for this initiative?	5
Barefoot Impact	3

R – Reposition

When you ask a business owner what their secret to success is, you will almost always hear something about the people that work with them. "Get the right people in the right seats" is a common term in the business world, but what does it actually mean? The "right people" component refers to employees who embrace your business's fundamental values and proactively help to create a corporate culture based on those values, as taken from Jim Collins' first best-selling book *Good to Great*.

Because having the wrong person in the wrong seat for a lengthy period can have negative consequences for company performance, all employees at every level must be evaluated before embarking on a bold endeavor and repositioned as needed.

Employees can be repositioned in two ways:

1. Promoted to a role that matches their current skillset and capacity.
2. Moved into a role that better fits their current skillset and capacity.

All employees fit into one of the following categories:

- Good fit for company culture/Highly skilled at their job (GF/HS)
- Good fit for company culture/Poor performance at their job (GF/PP)
- Poor fit for company culture/Highly skilled at their job (PF/HP)
- Poor fit for company culture/Poor performance at their job (PF/PP)

Note: Employees who are considered GF/HS or GF/PP are the only considerations for repositioning. Any employee who is a poor fit for the company culture may be more of a detriment than an asset no matter how well they perform.

Step 1 – Evaluate Every Employee

Each manager at every level should evaluate their direct reports using the criteria outlined above. Everyone in the organization should be classified and rated according to their department. You'll have a holistic perspective of your workforce once you've collected all of the replies, and you'll be able to utilize this knowledge to make future choices and actions.

Example (with fictional names)

Department	Name	GF/HS	GF/PP	PF/HP	PF/PP
Marketing	Suzie Hammond	x			
Marketing	Johnny Smith		x		
Marketing	Billy McNorth	x			
Operations	Jane Williams				x
Operations	Peter West	x			
Operations	Paulette Jones	x			

*In this case, the company realized that while Johnny was not very great at marketing, he was extremely organized and always made the effort to record and operationalize their procedures. He was not a suitable match for his present position, but he was moved into the operations department since he could offer value and fit the culture. Jane resigned after realizing she was not a suitable fit for her present position.

Step 2 – Evaluate Strategic Initiatives for the Next Year

It is critical not only to have the right people in the right seats but also to have them in the right seat at the right time. Various skill sets may be required depending on your present initiatives. If your department's main aim is innovation, for example, you'll want to make sure there are enough individuals on the team and/or that the leader has the capacity to satisfy the demand. Similarly, if another department has objectives that require structure, you'll want to make sure the team and leader are prepared.

Most initiatives will fit under one of four categories:

- Innovation – Creative initiatives that are either risky or rewarding
- Employee Experience – Collaborative team efforts that foster teamwork, conflict resolution, and serving one another with empathy
- Process Improvement – Implementation of processes or systems that promote compliance
- Results – Use data to inform decisions, decide on tactics, and take action to achieve desired outcomes

In this step, list out the department, the key initiative for the next year, and then categorize the initiative as described.

Example

Dept.	Key Initiative	Innovation	Emp. Exp.	Process Improvement	Results
Marketing	Improve retention by x percent		x		
Marketing	Investigate and implement new CRM solution to begin tracking the customer journey	x			
Marketing	Implement three initiatives to improve department morale		x		
Operations	Document current processes and start a company knowledge-base			x	
Operations	Achieve KPIs				x
Operations	Create an operational dashboard that shows status for all KPIs				x

Step 3 – Coach Staff As Needed

- If you have any doubts about an employee's competence, give them the benefit of the doubt and assume they are the correct person but in the wrong seat. Before determining that someone is not the perfect fit for the team, give them an opportunity to show themselves in another area.

- Make certain that an employee's direct manager has communicated expectations to them if they are under-performing. The manager should set explicit targets, be precise about the performance gap, provide a timeframe for improvement (for example, thirty days), and document the discussion.

- Do not spend *all* your time with underperforming staff. High-performing team members need guidance as well. If you neglect to intentionally develop your top performers, you may lose them to another company.

Step 4 – Evaluate Behavioral Assessments

In Chapter 4, we discussed how to use behavioral evaluations to better understand employee motivations, find the ideal person for the job, and provide coaching support. If you have already administered assessments to your employees, compare their results with your upcoming initiatives to help with decision-making.

Here are a few of the most frequently used behavioral evaluations:

- The Predictive Index
- DiSC Profile
- The Myers-Briggs Personality Type Indicator

- The Enneagram
- The MBS Survey

Step 5 – Evaluate Decisions and Act

Make the best choice for the company and the individual based on all of the facts acquired during this process. Employees should be *repositioned* as needed.

E – Execute

Starting with the first step and then assessing many elements, the plan will become evident—you'll see the whole image of what you have and require at this time. When you have all of this information in front of you, you can connect the dots and determine which sections of the company are affected and related. That is how you come up with a good strategy. Once you have this strategy, you can *execute it.*

It's not simple to make adjustments in a business that's already up and operating. You won't know how such changes will influence the organization and its overall performance unless you have the full picture in front of you. You will be able to propose an original solution and effectively execute your strategy once you have considered all of the factors.

The true job is putting your plans into action. I understand that developing a strategy requires a great deal of study, assessment, and thought, but your preparation will be for naught if you fail to carry it out correctly. As previously said, it is critical to ensure that any change in your company occurs at all levels. But how do you do that? How do you ensure the plan is executed at all levels? The answer is simple: change management.

You must establish clear priorities and take action to carry them out. You can't just instruct your employees to make the necessary modifications. You must develop techniques, processes, and plans to guarantee that new strategies are implemented. To effectively navigate through change, every one of your employees must understand the significance of change and incorporate it into their job. Here are the steps you need to take:

1. Set annual, quarterly, monthly, and weekly goals and track progress.
2. To be ready for inquiries, ensure that all executives are on board with the changes and understand the "why."
3. Ensure all managers and leaders understand the strategic intent, the "why," and have departmental goals tied to the major objective.
4. Ensure all staff members understand the strategic intent, the "why," and have personal goals tied to the major objective.
5. Require each leader to meet with each member of their team on a weekly or biweekly basis to discuss progress toward departmental and/or individual objectives.
6. Hold leaders accountable by utilizing performance assessments and incentives for achieving specified goals.
7. Check in on your objectives frequently to make sure you're on track. During status updates, be precise in your outcomes and ask probing questions.
8. Before you execute, run every goal, action, and obstacle you believe needs addressed through the following filter:
   a. Is it aligned with your company's BHAG?

b. Is it moving you closer to or further away from your BHAG?

c. Are you going to make money or lose money doing it?

d. Is it necessary?

e. Is it something you're already good at or will there be unnecessary ramp-up time?

f. Do you have the right people in the right seats to get the job done right?

Note: Read Chapter 7 to learn more about how change management influences the successful execution of the plan.

F – Follow–Up

Follow-up is the next important step. To keep an eye on the "pulse" of your major projects and the company as a whole, you'll need to plan recurring meetings. When you implement a new process or introduce a new system, it takes a lot of effort to make sure all things are on track and going as planned. *Follow-up* does not end. You may not need to supervise the ongoing processes after a while as much as you need to at the initial stages, but to keep things running smoothly, you need to ensure effective communication among employees and leaders.

Follow-up needs a system of accountability to ensure everything goes as planned. Without continual communication, you won't know if your plans are being executed as planned or if you need to make a change to make them better.

It is also important to arrange regular meetings for leaders, managers, and employees so they do not lose touch with the organizational goals and objectives. In a way, it works as a reinforcement and guide. Regular meetings help your teams remain attentive towards their responsibilities and keep different departments in sync with the organizational vision and strategic plan.

Over time, your employees, teams, and other leaders can veer off course, which can lead to disastrous effects on your organization. That is why it's important to gather your employees periodically for different meetings. In each meeting, ensure you deliver what is decided, what needs to be done, and who is responsible for what and when. Your meetings should make major goals of the company salient to ensure effective implementation of the changes.

Types of Recurring Meetings Needed

- Executive-level meeting for every member of the C-suite to update one another on key initiatives and KPIs, discuss risks, brainstorm solutions, and promote accountability.
- Project management update meeting hosted by the project management team to give leadership a high-level overview of the key project status, risks, and mitigations.
- Cross-departmental leadership meeting for managers and directors. Update one another on key initiatives and KPIs, discuss risks, brainstorm solutions, and promote accountability.
- Department meeting to keep staff updated on department metrics and informed of major changes and provide a space for them to share ideas.

- Company-wide meeting to keep all staff updated and informed on all cross-departmental initiatives, company projects, KPI status updates, and also provide a space for them to share ideas.

Note: Except for company-wide meetings, which should be conducted quarterly, many of these meetings should be held weekly or biweekly. However, use your own discretion.

Meeting Requirements

Meetings are an important part of every successful business. The important thing is that the meetings are successful, which means that they are productive. I hear a lot of executives complain about how many meetings they have and how much time they spend, but when I dig further, I find that the problem is that there is no framework in place for how the meeting should be run. The majority of the time, attendees leave meetings ignorant of what was discussed, making it difficult—if not impossible—to achieve significant objectives.

Regardless of the type of agenda you decide on, each recurrent meeting must satisfy the following conditions to be effective and get you closer to your objectives:

- All attendees should be informed of the topic of the meeting, the goal of the meeting, and why they are invited.
- All participants must know the purpose of the meeting series as well as the expected outcome for each meeting.

- All pre-read information, including the agenda, should be shared at least three days prior to the meeting day to allow appropriate prep time.
- All participants should be encouraged to share their thoughts and ideas during the meeting. Allow everyone the freedom to change directions, divert a subject, or park a conversation to keep the meeting on track toward its intended goal.
- The meeting should always start and end on time.
- Invite the participants who can make the necessary decisions.
- Send out a recap after each meeting that includes discussion points, who said they would do what by when, and any follow-up topics that will carry over to the next meeting.
- Start each meeting with a brief recap of what was covered previously and restate the desired outcome to ensure you stay on track.

O – Operationalize

You have identified goals, created a thorough action plan to meet them, and established the accountability framework. Now it is critical that you operationalize your plan. When you operationalize something, it means you have put it into action or use. So how can you *operationalize* your strategic plan? You must make the plan a living, breathing part of your company's operations. Strategic planning is the backbone of any organization, from the C-suite to the frontline staff, when done correctly. This means that all groups participate in the decision-making process.

Step 1 – Assign a Project Manager

A good strategic plan becomes a project-management system in the organization. The leadership schedules the work necessary to fulfill the tasks in the plan. They track the metrics that indicate the value of the strategic work they're doing, ensure that it's moving them closer to the vision and the intended year-end state, and make modifications as needed.

Step 2 – Ensure Everyone is Engaged

To be operationalized, the strategy must engage the whole organization, not just the C-suite. When the plan is finished, the top-level initiatives are turned into actions, which are then transmitted down to departments. Everyone understands how their individual responsibilities contribute to the master plan's success. This includes the following:

- Deliver project updates in company and department meetings.
- Assign individuals in all departments goals that are related to this major project.
- Keep track of progress at a micro- and macro-level with the master project plan.
- Celebrate wins along the journey.

Step 3 – Align Every Decision with Opportunities and Risks

An operationalized strategy aids management in making informed decisions regarding their time and resources. All operations should be assessed against, linked with, and driven by the strategic plan, which determines the direction. When a new opportunity or risk arises, ask the following questions:

- What role does this new opportunity play in our long-term strategy?
- How does this opportunity help us achieve our year-end goal?
- Does this opportunity align with our mission and progress us toward our goals?
- What happens if we do nothing about this risk?
- What is the potential impact of this risk if left unaddressed?

Step 4 – Revise the Plan as Needed

An operationalized plan is revised on a regular basis to ensure that it accurately reflects the strategic work being done. Here are questions to ask frequently to help guide your decisions and actions:

- Is it necessary to alter or reassign tasks to ensure that the work is completed?
- Do you require a new project or strategy to make the most of the opportunities presented by changes in technology or industry?
- Are your measurements indicating that you're still on track, or do you need to make some adjustments to your strategy to meet the goal condition?

Note: Operationalizing your strategy is a means of handling your strategic plan throughout the year that makes it an intrinsic part of your choices rather than a one-time fix.

O – Opportunities

Many individuals are apprehensive about change. That's reasonable given how many large corporations have been affected by such developments and have lost their market share. However, there is another angle to consider. Changes do not bring with them dangers; they bring with them possibilities. It is your responsibility as a leader to seek out and grasp such chances. Remember the BHAG goal you're working toward? The only way to achieve it is to innovate, enter new markets, and experience exponential growth. In the finding *opportunities* stage, you can start by brainstorming possible opportunities, keeping in mind different factors such as economic trends, market trends, changing relationships with stakeholders, as well as shifts in your target audience. To conduct a thorough analysis, there are four ways you can identify the best business opportunities:[27]

1. **Survey Current Customers**

   Listen to what consumers have to say about your industry, goods, and services when you're conversing with them. What are the most common questions you get? Experiences? Frustrations? What are their suggestions and gripes? This crucial consumer data may assist you in identifying significant business possibilities to expand and improve your present products and services.

2. **Survey Potential Clients and Past Leads**

Learn from potential consumers' requirements, wants, difficulties, and disappointments with your industry while you're targeting. Have they ever utilized comparable products and services? What did they enjoy and what did they despise? What brought them to you? What are their qualms about your goods or services? This will assist you in identifying chances to build more customized products and services, narrowing down your target market, and identifying and overcoming frequent obstacles.

3. **Research Competitors**

   See what other businesses are up to and, more importantly, what they aren't up to. Where are they collapsing? What exactly are they doing correctly? What draws customers to them rather than you? Researching your competition will assist you in identifying crucial business possibilities to broaden your market reach and improve your products and services.

4. **Analyze Industry Trends and Key Insights**

   Subscribe to industry magazines, join relevant organizations, set up Google alerts for important industry phrases and news, and follow other industry professionals on social media. Immerse yourself in your field and stay up-to-date on the newest techniques and trends.

T – Timeline

Whenever I am on a long road trip, I always have two questions:

1. Are we delayed?
2. What time will we arrive?

Knowing the answers to these questions allows me to evaluate whether I need to make any further stops and to set reasonable expectations. Because achieving a goal that will take more than ten years is a comparable journey, it's crucial that everyone involved understands the timeline, both for the reasons indicated above and to keep people interested in the strategic plan's key milestones and accomplishments.

A strategic plan is not the same as a business plan. Your strategic plan serves as a road map for getting from where you are to where you want to go. Every aspect of your strategy has a function in defining that trip. You are not explaining your business to the reader as you would in a business plan. The plan is only read by you, your employees, and your board of directors and must include a *time* component to measure whether you are on track.

Therefore, allow your BHAG to be the driving force behind your three- to five-year and annual plans. To guarantee that you can accomplish your objective and keep your team unified behind its long-term strategic vision, every year, every milestone, and every significant project should have a clear link to your BHAG.

> "To begin with the end in mind means to start with a clear understanding of your destination. It means to know where you're going so that you better understand where you are now and so that the steps you take are always in the right direction."
>
> —Stephen R. Covey

The Timeline

1. Create a timeline that has your BHAG listed at the end of it. Include the year you will reach it.
2. Every three to five years on the timeline, write three to five goals you will need to reach to achieve the BHAG.
3. At the beginning of the timeline, write three to five goals that must be completed within the next six months to stay on track with your next major milestones.

Note: This framework should be revisited during your annual planning and adjusted as needed. Your annual and quarterly goals will be birthed out of this document.

Accountability

Given how competitive a market may become, you can't afford to be late in putting your plans into action and introducing your products and services. If you don't meet your deadlines, your competitors will gain an advantage. Therefore, as you go through each process, double-check that everything has a start and end time. You'll need a mechanism in place to hold people responsible for their actions.

You must have a system to hold people accountable for their responsibilities and get things done promptly. It should be obvious who is responsible for what and when, and a timetable with milestones and deadlines can help with this. This will assist you in not just gaining momentum, but also in tracking your progress.

Conclusion

This BAREFOOT method is a very effective framework for systematically completing tasks. While the steps are not sequential, each phase must be evaluated to ensure success. The ultimate objective is to assist you in achieving your Big Hairy Audacious Goal. This entire process will take one to three years, and you should revisit it frequently as you work toward your ten- to twenty-five-year goal. If any aspect is neglected, it can influence business and its long-term plans.

Note: Visit www.xposeyoursolutions.com for information about our BAREFOOT leadership certifications and training options.

Phase 3

Stand on the Table

Chapter 7

Effective Change Management

"As dealing with change becomes a regular activity, leading it becomes a skill to hone, an internal capacity to master."
Arnaud Henneville

Imagine you are in a meeting with the entire leadership team. You are not just in the meeting; you are conducting the meeting. At some point during your presentation, you decide to take your shoes off. You not only take your shoes off, but you choose to stand on the table. Now you are standing on top of a table, presenting to your peers with no socks or shoes on. You are barefoot! How does that feel? How do the other professionals in the meeting perceive you? What thoughts cross your mind? Are you able to stay focused on the main objective while others are staring at you? Because I am sure all the other executives would be staring at you.

This behavior would grab their attention because it's not the norm. The first thing in their mind would be, *why would you take your shoes off?* They would likely be distracted.

When you take unconventional actions in hopes of getting an extraordinary outcome, the responses are similar. As a leader, you must have the courage to take such steps—to be "barefoot"—so that you can do whatever is necessary to achieve your most audacious goals. You must be willing to stand out and do things differently than others would. After all, someone must go against the norm to ensure your organization has longevity.

> *Whenever you are given a seat at the table, don't sit. Stand.*

Often, leaders are happy with just having a seat at the table. However, having a seat at the table where decision-making happens means nothing if everyone is committed to doing what they have always done.

> *No matter what the situation is, if you have the authority to lead, do not sit. STAND.*

- **S**elfless – Acting in the best interests of others rather than oneself.
- **T**actful – Diplomatic; capable of conveying criticism without upsetting or hurting others.
- **A**ware – Having a particular interest in or experience with something, and hence being up-to-date with current events in that field.
- **N**imble – Quick to comprehend, think, invent, and so forth.
- **D**aring – Courageous or audaciously bold.

When you STAND as a leader, you demand respect and accept responsibility for bringing about essential changes for the organization's growth and development. It conveys that it is not about exploiting the authority you have, but about bringing innovation, development, and implementation of plans under your supervision. Leaders who take a STAND and are willing to work barefoot on the table will be able to navigate their organizations as long as they understand and implement the main ingredient to success: change management.

Change management is at the heart of a company's ability to accept and implement change successfully. It enables employees to comprehend and commit to the shift while also allowing them to perform efficiently. Effective change management is vital to fundamental transformation. Many organizations spend substantial time and valuable resources to improve their functions, but not many succeed in integrating new practices into organizational routines. It is understandable given that no matter how significant the change is, it should incorporate the standard workflow of the organization, and that is not an easy task to do. If you want to implement the BAREFOOT method mentioned in the next chapter, you need to evaluate your organization's capacity to adapt to changes in your organization.

Have you ever set out to operationalize a brilliant new business practice, only to discover that the idea was no longer brilliant once it got past the leadership level? That is because it takes time to prepare your employees and systems to be ready for changes. You cannot expect them to accept changes overnight. When you foresee that your organization will need to revise its practices, you must ensure that your employees are ready for it and will not resist the change. This will help you implement your new strategies and plans by increasing the capacity to integrate them and put forward the routinizing phase where new techniques will occur.

> *When you can speak intelligently about the progress, potential problems, and proactive measures being taken, you build trust with your teams.*

It is your responsibility to take the initiative to motivate your team and show them the way toward improvement, seizing opportunities, and tackling key issues that need to be addressed. These changes I am referring to require a perception change. You should be able to see things from different angles. These include changes to job roles, processes, organizational structures, and new technologies. Although it is a two-way process, your leadership and guidance for effective transitions will only work when you take a STAND.

- Be selfless by making the best decisions for the team and the organization, not yourself.
- Be tactful in your approach. Consider how the changes impact those you are communicating with and convey all messages with empathy and in a timely fashion.
- Be aware of why the changes are being made, the expected benefits, and stay updated. When you can speak intelligently about the progress, potential problems, and proactive measures being taken, you build trust with your teams.
- Be nimble in your thinking. You must be quick to comprehend, ask for clarification, think, invent, and come up with solutions.
- Be daring enough to have unpopular, yet necessary, conversations, and courageous enough to overcome resistance until you get the desired result.

Implement and Design Winning Teams

The announcement is the easy part; it makes the manager look bold and decisive. Implementation is more difficult, because no matter how good and compelling the data, there will always be active and passive resistance, rationalizations, debates, and distractions—particularly when the changes require new ways of working or painful cuts. To get through this, managers have to get their

> hands dirty, engage their teams to make choices, and
> sometimes confront recalcitrant colleagues.
>
> —Ron Ashkenas and Rizwan Khan

Every employee has a unique role to play in aiding transformation within a business. While many employees may perform meticulous work, top leaders with more experience may have distinct objectives. Even within management, there are differences in the duties that leaders and managers undertake. For example, leaders will communicate the vision for the change, while managers will take responsibility for determining the process for the change and implementing it with their teams. Top leaders and managers must work together to involve all employees in the plans to be effective.

Employees are one of the most critical assets. You need to align your innovation and desire for change with the company's overall strategy and communicate that to your teams. That way your team will have a clear understanding of new goals. To effectively implement new methods and processes, establish a good-governance practice, monitor it, evaluate the results, and make necessary adjustments when and where needed.

Since your employees need to focus most on implementing changes, you need to work towards improving your workforce and their productivity. One important thing to note here is that a leader must focus on internal and external talent when preparing human resources for future needs. Using these resources, you must know how you will attract, train, and retain the best people you can find. That's because the successful innovation of your company depends on the quality of the innovation team you build.

Another thing you need to acknowledge is that even though you are a leader, you must train your teams to be autonomous. This does not mean you won't supervise or guide them. When you routinize new practices, it simply means teaching employees to take control over the daily operations in the future. This is very important to consider if your goals are to integrate new practices fast and effectively to get a high-quality outcome.

Introducing New Practices and Implementing Changes

Introducing new practices and implementing changes requires a leader to facilitate the plans. For visible improvements in outcomes, the commitment of the leaders of the organization and training personnel plays a significant role. These are the people who must form organizational culture and group dynamics, making it easier to integrate new practices in a running company.

It is imperative to note a strong connection between the effectiveness of implementation and the climate for implementation of the new practices. What you need to do as a leader is plan for the implementation of your goals. While you do so, keep in mind that it is natural for people to resist organizational changes.

You cannot expect your teams and employees to adapt to changes right away. As a leader, you always need to plan. If you believe your company will need to change its structure and practices, start preparing your employees as you devise your plans for the organization's future.

As you work on your planned changes, slowly and gradually work on creating a climate for the implementation that encompasses organizational policies, practices, and social norms that support the innovation and its use. This way, it will be easier to implement new methods and changes as your teams will be prepared; the changes will be more appealing to them. Having your employees prepared in advance will also encourage them to help modify procedures to accommodate the differences better.

Change Management and Implementation

Changes are inevitable. There is no way to avoid changes. The only way to tackle changes is by managing them. With good change management, you can create an environment and system that helps the employees. The business will be able to adapt to the changes and embrace the new way of working.

The Four Principles of Change Management

For good change management, a leader must know and follow four core principles:[18]

- Understand Change
- Plan Change
- Implement Change
- Communicate Change

Understand Change

You must understand a change first before doing anything about it. Unless you know what you are facing, you cannot prepare for it properly. As a result, all of your efforts will be in vain. While you analyze a situation, look at the bigger picture to understand the connection between the change and your organization. This will let you figure out how the change is going to impact your organization. Think about the following questions:

- What are the changes you need to make? What can you do to make people adapt to it and successfully achieve the change?
- Why is this change required? How does it impact your objectives? Given the changing circumstances, what are your key objectives?
- What benefits can this change bring to the organization?
- How can you benefit from this change and impact people positively?
- How is it going to change the system of your organization and environment? Does it require your employees to change the way they work?

It is also essential to look the other way and think about its impact if you do not make the required changes. This way, you will know that the change is necessary for the survival of the organization. Hence, you will be confident about the new approach.

Plan Change

The second principle is to plan the change. Now that you know what you are facing and why the change is essential, you need to figure out the best approach to design it. The very first thing you need to tell yourself is that an effective change won't happen by chance.

You will need to analyze several factors carefully and devise the most effective plan for your organization. It is crucial to go through each element as every organization is different, and the impact of any change varies from organization to organization. You will need to see if your organization's structure and the nature of the business allow for a flexible approach or if you will need to stick to a rigid one.

However, some questions can help you consider a plan, such as:

- Do you have resources and high-level support to sponsor the change? If yes, how can you secure, engage, and use them?
- What do you think are the best resources/support you have that can help the organization's current situation? Do you have enough internal resources to support the change, or will you need external expertise?
- How can you win support from people across the business? Do you have adequate means to do that?
- Picture what you want to achieve. What do you think the outcome should look like?
- What are the change goals you plan to achieve?

- How can you predict and assess the impact of the changes you are planning to make?
- How will you measure your success?

These questions will allow you to see where you stand and where you want to be. Moreover, they will help you utilize your current resources in the best way possible.

Implement Change

Now that you have a plan, it's time to execute it. Implementing a project is much more complicated than devising the project itself. That's because if you do not use the right strategy, it will not work the way you expected. There is no strict rule regarding what approach you should use. As I said, every organization is different, and as a leader, you must know what works best for your organization.

You need to focus on two main areas: how fast the organization needs to adapt to change, and being mindful of people's feelings during the implementation of those changes. For example, if there is a need for urgency, yet you want to build the momentum along the way, Kotter's eight-step change model can help you implement the change in such situations. Using the Change Curve, you can also understand how people adapt to changes as they go through different stages.[19]

Several strategies and tools can help implement changes, but whichever you choose, the following steps can help you to implement change:

- Ensure everyone understands the plan's what, why, and how.
- Make sure to conduct a regular assessment of the changes to see if the plan works, then make changes to the plan as required.
- To determine the level of involvement, identify all your stakeholders and map them. This way, you will know who is affected most by the changes.
- Identify the training needs of employees to implement changes.
- You can also resort to professional help. Appoint change agents who understand the process and help to implement new practices and procedures.
- Find ways to engage employees in new practices so that they adapt to them quickly and change them into the norm.

During the implementation of your plan, consider a cadence. Make sure you conduct short and frequent meetings to evaluate the change and increase the work momentum. When you keep updating the teams on progress and the next steps, it boosts their morale and makes the adaptation process a bit easier.

Communicate Change

If you fail to communicate effectively with your employees, the change you seek will be a far-fetched dream. Additionally, you need to ensure the way you communicate is encouraging and powerful.

An effective way of communicating creates a shared sense and vision of the future. It helps people in the organization feel like a part of something meaningful. It inspires them to do their best. If you want the change management plans to be effective, you must consider good stakeholder management. That helps you determine the best possible way to communicate the right message to the right people, which has a massive impact on their involvement in changes.[20]

A leader should address a few things in their communication, but if they find communication tricky, specific tools can help them.

The ADKAR change management model is quite a helpful tool that helps leaders communicate their change by assisting them to focus on the crucial areas such as:[21]

- **A**wareness – Focus your message on the need for change.
- **D**esire – Trigger the desire to participate and support a change. Figure out what encourages employees to adopt changes.
- **K**nowledge – Communicate the processes and provide tools to help employees understand how to change.
- **A**bility – Focus on the employees' ability to change. See what skills they have that can help the employees change and work in a new way. Do they have the potential to learn and grow?
- **R**einforcement – When people start adapting to changes, make sure they stick to that. Reinforce using different strategies to sustain a change in the long run.

Change management does not end, even when the change is complete. You must continually analyze outcomes, collect data, train staff on new techniques and business processes, and revise targets as needed throughout and after the process.

If your organization is embarking on large-scale changes with the BAREFOOT Method™, you may need to interchange various methodologies in conjunction with it. In my experience, there is no one-size-fits-all solution. I highly recommend reviewing the list below (in no particular order), investigating the advantages and disadvantages, determining which one complements your strategy best, and then working with a professional to operationalize the framework(s) of your choice.

- The McKinsey 7-S model
- Kotter's change management theory
- ADKAR change management model
- Nudge theory
- Lewin's change management model
- The Satir change management methodology
- Bridges' transition model

Note: It is possible to use any of these methods, or others, to manage change effectively. This list is not comprehensive as I only documented the ones I am familiar with. Remember—always take a STAND while barefoot!

Chapter 8

Trust the Process

"Here's to the crazy ones, the misfits, the rebels, the troublemakers, the round pegs in the square holes . . . the ones who see things differently—they're not fond of rules. . . . You can quote them, disagree with them, glorify or vilify them, but the only thing you can't do is ignore them, because they change things . . . they push the human race forward, and while some may see them as the crazy ones, we see genius, because the ones who are crazy enough to think that they can change the world are the ones who do."
Steve Jobs

The words quoted above are from one of the most renowned personalities in technology, Steve Jobs. He truly believed that success only happens by breaking the rules that don't serve the organization's primary purpose. I've never personally met Steve. However, I have met many "troublemaking" leaders who see things differently, challenge the status quo, and produce exceptional results. I won't list them all, but I will take a moment to tell you about three who fit this description.

Mitch McLeod

Several years ago, I had the privilege of not only working for a successful start-up but also meeting one of the most brilliant leaders I know, Mitch McLeod, the founder. He started ARCOS LLC, a critical infrastructure industry software solution, in 1993. The applications enable clients such as utility providers, transportation companies, power plants, airlines, and the like to respond to crises, track and schedule personnel and resources, restore services faster, report in real-time, and give step-by-step replays of critical milestones after they have occurred. He is definitely one of the "crazy ones, the misfits, the rebels, the troublemakers, the round pegs in the square holes . . . the ones who see things differently." Since its inception, ARCOS has grown from less than five employees to about one-hundred-fifty. The company earned Columbus Business First's Fast 50 award every year from 2007 through 2014—an annual rating of the fifty fastest-growing young firms in central Ohio. The award honors firms annually for their financial growth and success over the previous three years. To date, the company has been around for about twenty-eight years and continues to expand through strategic acquisitions, partnerships, and innovation. In the time that I worked at ARCOS LLC, I was exposed to various aspects of the business, working closely with the executive team to scale the services and support department for the tremendous growth experienced. As a result, I experienced tremendous growth.

During one of our annual conferences, I sat with Mitch for about an hour as he allowed me to pick his brain. I was interested in his journey as an entrepreneur and his steps to success. He shared the story of how he almost went bankrupt in the beginning and had to make some pivotal changes to stay in business. Once he got through that difficult time and refined his niche in 2005, the business began to skyrocket. There were six things that stood out to me from our conversation:

1. He had a clear vision and a plan to achieve it.
2. He prioritized customer feedback to drive innovation.
3. He made tough decisions and broke organizational norms.
4. He focused on hiring the right people.
5. He was motivated by building sincere relationships instead of making money.
6. He trusted the process.

Forbes Riley

Last year during the COVID-19 pandemic, I had the chance to meet and receive personal coaching from Forbes Riley. I met her backstage during a virtual event we both spoke at. During our session, she asked me a question that changed the trajectory of my life. She asked me, "Shara, what do you want?" I gave some generic answers, and then she followed up by asking, "What do you really want?" At that moment, I felt like a lump was in my throat because I realized that even though many already saw me as a success, I had greater potential. She helped me know that I can have so much more as long as I ask for it.

Until that day, I did not know who she was, and now that I've learned more about her, I'll never forget her. Forbes Riley, a celebrity life coach, is undoubtedly charismatic in front of a crowd. I have heard others refer to her as the female Tony Robbins. She is a pioneer of infomercials, home shopping, and creator of the Spin Gym. Despite personal tragedies and challenges, she became the CEO of a multimillion-dollar fitness company. She lives by her own mantra: "You are the sum of the obstacles you overcome."

I consider her a barefoot leader, not just because she took her shoes off at a conference where she spoke in front of over ten thousand people because her feet were hurting, but because she has been a trailblazer in her industry. Before publishing this book, I contacted her for an interview to understand how she evolved to where she is now in her career. She graciously accepted. I asked her several questions, but I will share two responses:

Note: To listen to the entire interview, visit the *Barefoot in the Boardroom* podcast on any major platform.

1. **Considering all you've accomplished, what are you most proud of?**

   Forbes is most proud of her children. She is currently in business with her eighteen-year-old daughter, who grossed almost one million dollars in a year during the COVID-19 pandemic. Forbes discussed how she introduced her children to the world and taught them business principles while they were still young. And rather than pushing them away due to her hectic schedule, she took them along. She took them on business trips to Europe and China. She admitted that, despite her many achievements, she had been unhappy at numerous periods during her life. She learned that money cannot buy happiness and that spending quality time with family and friends is essential. She is now content and enjoying the life she has always desired. The lesson here is that no matter how successful you are in business, you must prioritize those who mean the most to you. Make an investment in yourself, your children, and your future. If you do this, you will get a positive return on investment.

2. **What advice would you give to any leader who's afraid to step out of their comfort zone and walk "barefoot" to get to their next level?**

She told the story of how her daughter asked the question: "All the good stuff lives on the other side of fear, how come nobody seems to know that?" Forbes replied, "Because they didn't have me as a mother." She discussed how we are conditioned to be fearful by the time we graduate elementary school, but that we must reprogram our minds in order to get the results we want. You've probably asked for permission one-hundred-thousand times as a kid and been told no the same number of times. This teaches you to raise your hand before acting, but if you want to achieve big things, you can't wait for someone to say yes. You must be willing to break the rules to succeed. When Forbes hears the word "no," that translates in her mind to "never-ending opportunity." The takeaway here is that if you want to be an innovator, you can't wait for permission to take difficult but essential action; you have to bring the right ideas to the table first. You must see a "never-ending opportunity" when others see a "no."

I consider both Mitch and Forbes geniuses because they are two of the ones who were "crazy enough to think that they could change the world"—and they have and are continuing to do so.

You

The third person I would classify as one of the leaders Steve Jobs described in the quote mentioned above is *you*. You are a "square peg in a round hole" who walks barefoot, stands on the table, and drives transformation. However, because change is unavoidable and ongoing, you must constantly push yourself to new heights. It's easy to get caught up in yesterday's accomplishments and stay there, but scaling for the future necessitates asking yourself good questions regularly.

Here are some examples:

- When was the last time you looked beyond the boundaries of organizational rules and made a significant impact that you can quantify?
- When was the last time you took uncomfortable action?

- When was the last time you intentionally took yourself off "autopilot" and did something other than what you've always done to solve a problem?
- When was the last time you challenged the organizations' vision to ensure everyone's alignment with the purpose or that the purpose still fits the strategic direction?

These are not rhetorical questions. Would you please take a moment to reflect and then answer them? *Pause.*

If your answer to all four questions is anything other than today, you may be too fond of rules to stir up enough trouble to start a real revolution. You may be comfortable right where you are, doing what you are doing and not working towards reaching your fullest potential. However, if you are still reading this book, I know three things about you:

1. You have an audacious goal (as described in earlier chapters).
2. You have all the tools necessary to reach your audacious goal.
3. You are willing to try unconventional methods to achieve your audacious goal.

Throughout my leadership journey, I have been able to meet—and even exceed—some pretty outstanding objectives. I have had the opportunity to help organizations overcome many obstacles, forge through limitations, develop scalable processes, and build high-performing teams that propelled them to the next level. However, in the spirit of being "barefoot in the boardroom" and breaking all the rules to get my point across, I will not use a professional story to conclude this book, but rather a personal one to illustrate my closing thoughts.

Trust the Process

It took my husband and me eight years and over seven hundred needles to have our son. Having a child was one of our audacious goals. It was considered audacious because I was diagnosed with infertility. We had all of the right "tools," meaning our reproductive cells were in the normal range. However, the proper connection could not be made without intervention. After eight years of wondering if I would ever be a mom, four in vitro fertilization (IVF) transfers (an investment of over $55,000), various protocols, and multiple surgeries as well as losses along the journey, we had our little miracle. There were times I felt like it would never happen for me, but after every obstacle, every disappointment, I continued to say, "*But*, I still want to be a mom." Since I couldn't shake the feeling or desire, I kept pursuing it until what I spoke was in my hand. I had to trust the process. My son is my daily reminder that even when things don't look like what I say I want, if I hold on to hope and keep taking steps towards the goal, I will keep getting closer until I achieve the "impossible."

I want to take a moment to encourage you also to trust the process. When the dream you have is big enough to ensure your organization has longevity and your team scales to meet the demand, there will be times along the journey when you will wonder when you'll see tangible results. Change takes time, even when you have the right team in place and all the right tools. It is possible to have a fully functioning organizational structure and still need intervention. Just as I had to try various methods and procedures, experience setbacks, and make a significant investment to achieve the "impossible," you will too. When you feel discouraged, if you determine that you still want the result, you will achieve it as long as you keep taking steps in that direction. Trust the process.

> *"If you do not change direction,*
> *you may end up where you are heading."*
> Lao Tzu

Take the Steps

Like Steve Jobs said, the crazy ones have what it takes to change by taking steps that not many would. Many leaders are afraid to take the steps necessary to get to their next level for various reasons.

1. The next step will be risky. Where there is no risk there is no reward, so take it anyway.
2. The next step may be lonely. You must be willing to walk with or without those you thought would be with you.
3. The next step is costly. Giving up what you want for what you want more will be worth it.

Be that crazy one. Be brave enough to stand barefoot on the boardroom table and do whatever it takes to navigate your team through change.

Remember, it is not just about survival but about sustainability. Take control of the wheel of your leadership vehicle, avoid an organizational CRASH, steer in the direction of your most audacious goals, and navigate change until you arrive at the desired destination. In other words, take the steps to enter the boardroom, take off your shoes, and then STAND on the table!

About the Author

With a dual master's degree in business and ministry as well as a bachelor's degree in technical management, Shara Hutchinson is the CEO of Xposeyour. Shara is a TEDx speaker and international best-selling author, including being a co-author of *1 Habit of the World's Great Leaders: Life-Changing Habits to Unlock Your True Leadership Potential.* She is a technology-oriented executive and customer success professional with over seventeen years of leadership experience and a proven track record of developing and implementing operational strategies and technologies that creatively enhance the customer experience while supporting key business initiatives. Shara is a change agent with extensive experience delivering value and leveraging customer feedback to ensure long-term relationships that drive retention and recurring revenue expansion.

She has a specialty in transforming teams from the start-up phase to enterprise level by scaling processes to match growth and strengthening cohesion interdepartmentally. She is passionate about optimizing the customer experience to drive results, building high-performing, customer-centric teams by hiring right the first time, developing existing employees, and motivating professionals.

When Shara is not working, she spends time making memories with her husband of eleven years and her three-year-old miracle son, who took eight years and four IVF cycles to conceive. It was difficult for her to imagine being a mom during that journey, but after each obstacle, she kept trying until she achieved the desired result. As a result of this experience, Shara published *I STILL Want to Be a Mom: An Inspirational Guide to Help Women Struggling with Infertility* to help other women going through a similar struggle. When Shara wants something, she finds a way to achieve it. This tenacity applies to business results as well.

Websites:

www.xposeyoursolutions.com

www.sharahutchinson.com

References

1. MGI. (2021, December 21). "My Top 4 Tips to Future Proof Your Business." Retrieved from MGI: https://www.mginz.co.nz/growth/top-4-tips-future-proof-business/

2. Rhythm Systems. (2021, July 5). "How to Create Your BHAG - BIG HAIRY AUDACIOUS GOAL." Retrieved from Rhythm Systems: https://www.rhythmsystems.com/bhag-big-hairy-audacious-goal

3. Donnelly, C. (2020, December 21). "Failure to Innovate – Why Did Blockbuster Fail?" Retrieved from VERB: https://verbbrands.com/news/thoughts/failure-to-innovate-why-did-blockbuster-fail/

4. Surbhi, S. (2020, December 15). "Difference Between Leader and Manager." Retrieved from Key Difference:

https://keydifferences.com/difference-between-leader-and-manager.html

5. Hassell, B. (2020, December 12). "Leaders Need Exposure". Retrieved from Leadership Development: https://www.chieflearningofficer.com/2017/03/13/leaders-need-exposure/

6. See note 5 above.

7. Scott, T. (2020, May 18). "Every Leader Should S.W.O.T." Retrieved from Maximized Growth: https://www.tasham-scott.com/blog/swotthyself

8. Wowk, A. (2020, December 1). "6 Steps to Mapping the Employee Journey at Your Organization." Retrieved from Qualtrics: https://www.qualtrics.com/blog/employee-journey-mapping/

9. Solomon, Cindy. *The Rules of Woo: An Entrepreneur's Guide to Capturing the Hearts & Minds of Today's Customers.* New York: OPR Publishers, 2010.

10. Blake. (2020, January 22). "20 Fresh Examples Of Customer Experience Innovation." Retrieved from BlakeMorgan: https://www.blakemichellemorgan.com/blog/20-fresh-examples-customer-experience-innovation/

11. Gomez, J. G. (2017, November 20). "Customer Service: Is 'Underpromising and Overdelivering' Worth the Effort?" Retrieved from Open Access: https://www.openaccessbpo.com/blog/customer-service-underpromising-overdelivering-worth-effort/

12. Emerson, M. (2020, December 11). "How to Under Promise and Over Deliver to Your Customers." Retrieved from Nextiva: https://www.nextiva.com/blog/how-to-under-promise-and-overdeliver-to-your-customers.html

13. Smulski, J. (2021, January 12). "How to Track Your Customer's Journey." Retrieved from SherpaDesk: https://www.sherpadesk.com/blog/how-to-track-your-customers-journey

14. Wesley, C. (2021, July 19). "CRM (customer relationship management)." Retrieved from TechTarget: https://search-customerexperience.techtarget.com/definition/CRM-customer-relationship-management

15. See note 14 above.

16. Expert, E. H. (2018, June 26). "5 Ways to Measure Customer Experience." Retrieved from Engage Hub: https://engagehub.com/5-ways-to-measure-customer-experience/

17. Kramer, S. (2018, August 27). "10 Stats Linking Employee Experience with Customer Experience." Retrieved from Future of Work: https://fowmedia.com/stats-linking-employee-experience-to-customer-experience/

18. Ramos, D. (2016, December 14). "8 Elements of an Effective Change Management Process." Retrieved from Smartsheet: https://www.smartsheet.com/8-elements-effective-change-management-process

19. See note 18 above.

20. See note 18 above.

21. PROSCI. (2020, December 20). "What is Change Management?" Retrieved from PROSCI: https://www.prosci.com/resources/articles/what-is-change-management

22. APS. (2014, October 8). "Navigating Familiar Roads May Lead to Driving on 'Autopilot.'" Retrieved from APS: https://www.psychologicalscience.org/news/motr/navigating-familiar-roads-may-lead-to-driving-on-autopilot.html

23. See note 2 above.

24. See note 13 above.

25. See note 23 above.

26. See note 23 above.

27. Jesnoewki, A. (2018, November 20). "Four Ways to Identify More Business Opportunities." Retrieved from Smart Company: https://www.smartcompany.com.au/startupsmart/advice/business-planning/four-ways-to-identify-more-business-opportunities/

A free ebook edition is available with the purchase of this book.

To claim your free ebook edition:

1. Visit MorganJamesBOGO.com
2. Sign your name CLEARLY in the space
3. Complete the form and submit a photo of the entire copyright page
4. You or your friend can download the ebook to your preferred device

A **FREE** ebook edition is available for you
or a friend with the purchase of this print book.

CLEARLY SIGN YOUR NAME ABOVE

Instructions to claim your free ebook edition:
1. Visit MorganJamesBOGO.com
2. Sign your name CLEARLY in the space above
3. Complete the form and submit a photo of this entire page
4. You or your friend can download the ebook to your preferred device

Print & Digital Together Forever.

Snap a photo

Free ebook

Read anywhere